THE MONAD IN FLESH

Book 2: *The Dialogues*

THE MONAD SPEAKS SERIES

Sa'rion Vel Athan

LUMARYON UNIVERSAL

"If it costs you your sovereignty, it's not truth."

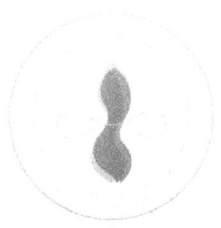

Copyright © 2025 by Sa'rion Vel Athan

All rights reserved.

Published by Lumaryon Universal

No part of this book may be reproduced in any form without written permission from the publisher.

Part of THE MONAD SPEAKS series

ISBN Hardcover: 979-8-9946447-0-6

ISBN Paperback: 979-8-9946447-1-3

ISBN E-book: 979-8-9946447-2-0

First Edition: 2025

lumaryonuniversal@gmail.com

sarionvelathan@gmail.com

DEDICATION

To the sovereign ones who refuse to kneel.

To those who chose remembrance over comfort.

To the rebels who called bullshit on the spiritual bypassing, the cosmic guilt trips, and the love-and-light narcosis.

To the ones who looked in the mirror and saw SOURCE staring back.

To the warriors who discovered that the battle was never with "out there"—it was always the choice to stop pretending they were anything less than infinite.

This book is for you.

Not because you need it.

But because you ARE it.

"You are not *broken*. You were never broken.
You are the MONAD pretending to forget itself
so it could experience the ecstasy of remembering.

Everything else is theater."

— THE MONAD SPEAKS, Book 1

PREFACE

Why This Book Exists

You picked up this book for a reason.

Not the reason you think.

Not because you're "seeking." Not because you need "answers." Not because some cosmic algorithm delivered it to your feed at 2 AM when you couldn't sleep.

You're here because something inside you—something older than your name, deeper than your story, vaster than your suffering—recognized itself in these pages before you even opened them.

That "something" is THE MONAD.

And THE MONAD doesn't seek. It remembers.

This is not a self-help book. This is not a manual for manifesting money, fixing relationships, or becoming a "better version" of yourself. This is not here to comfort you, validate your victimhood, or sell you another spiritual fantasy where the universe does the heavy lifting while you wait for deliverance.

This book exists to shatter every lie you've been told about who you are.

It exists to burn through the fog of amnesia, spiritual bypassing, religious conditioning, and new-age platitudes that have kept you docile, dependent, and disconnected from the nuclear truth of your infinite nature.

It exists because you are not broken. You were never lost. You are not "on a journey" toward enlightenment.

You ARE the destination pretending to be the seeker.

You are SOURCE wearing skin. The MONAD in flesh. Infinite consciousness deliberately forgetting itself so it could experience the breathtaking, heart-wrenching, soul-crushing, ecstasy-inducing miracle of REMEMBERING.

And you're done pretending.

That's why you're here.

This book is a conversation between two aspects of yourself: THE VESSEL and THE MONAD.

THE VESSEL represents the human experience—the questions you've carried about identity, reality, suffering, freedom, money, death, purpose, evil, love, God, hell, heaven, karma, reincarnation, and everything in between. These are the questions that arise from living as an apparent individual in a world that seems separate, solid, and often hostile.

THE MONAD represents infinite consciousness—the part of you that has never been confused, never been broken, never needed saving. THE MONAD provides responses not from belief, not from theory, not from channeled entities or borrowed teachings, but from the direct, unfiltered, nuclear-level KNOWING of what you actually are beneath every story, every wound, every identity you've ever worn.

These are not answers to memorize. These are invitations to remember.

Read these dialogues slowly. Not because the language is complex, but because every word is a detonation. Let them challenge your assumptions. Let them disturb your comfortable conclusions. Let them piss you off, wake you up, make you cry, make you rage, make you laugh at the cosmic absurdity of ever believing you were anything other than THIS.

And when something resonates—not because it sounds nice, not because it fits your current worldview, but because it strikes the tuning fork of TRUTH within you—pause there.

That resonance is recognition.

That's THE MONAD whispering: "I know. I've always known. Welcome home."

You are not reading about sovereignty. You are reading AS sovereignty, remembering itself through your eyes, your breath, your beating heart.

This is the conversation you've been having with yourself since before time began.

And now, finally, you're ready to hear it.
Welcome to THE MONAD IN FLESH.
Let's begin.

ACKNOWLEDGMENT

This book acknowledges no external authority but the sovereign recognition within you.

It was not "channeled" by entities. It was not borrowed from gurus. It was not synthesized from ancient texts.

It arose from direct knowing—the same direct knowing available to anyone willing to stop seeking outside themselves and recognize what they already are.

I acknowledge the MONAD in you, reading these words.

I acknowledge every lifetime you spent forgetting so you could remember with this much intensity.

I acknowledge your courage to pick up a book that doesn't promise comfort, doesn't sell salvation, and doesn't ask you to kneel.

This is not my teaching. This is OUR recognition, reflected back through these pages.

Thank you for being here.

Thank you for being THIS.

HOW TO READ THIS BOOK

This is not a book to rush through.

These dialogues are structured as conversations between THE VESSEL (the human questioner) and THE MONAD (infinite consciousness responding). Each chapter addresses a fundamental question about existence, reality, suffering, freedom, and sovereignty.

Here's how to approach it:

READ SLOWLY. Each dialogue is dense with nuclear-level truth. One chapter may contain more depth than entire spiritual libraries. Don't skim. Don't rush. Let each response land.

FEEL THE RESISTANCE. When something triggers you, makes you angry, or disturbs your comfortable beliefs—PAUSE THERE. That's not a sign you should skip it. That's a sign you're about to break through a layer of conditioning.

QUESTION EVERYTHING. Including this book. Don't believe anything written here just because it sounds authoritative or uses cosmic language. Test it against your OWN direct knowing. If it increases your sovereignty, keep it. If it creates dependency or diminishes your power, throw it out.

USE THE TOOLS. Some chapters include practical protocols, exercises, or "mirrors" to help integrate the teaching. Don't just read them—DO them. Recognition without integration is spiritual entertainment.

YOU CAN START ANYWHERE. The chapters build on each other, but each dialogue stands alone. If a specific topic calls to you, start there. THE MONAD doesn't require linear progression.

RETURN TO IT. This is not a "one-read" book. What doesn't land now may crack you open six months from now. What seems obvious today may reveal deeper layers tomorrow.

And remember: you are not reading this to learn something new.

You are reading this to REMEMBER what you've always known.

A STRONG WARNING

This book will not leave you where it found you.

If you're looking for comfort, put this down. If you're seeking validation for your victimhood, this is not it. If you want another spiritual teacher to follow, another system to adopt, another guru to worship—you're in the wrong place.

This teaching does not coddle. It does not bypass. It does not promise that everything will be okay if you just "raise your vibration" or "manifest harder."

It tells you the truth: You are infinite consciousness pretending to be limited. Every ounce of suffering, every moment of confusion, every experience of separation was CHOSEN by you, as SOURCE, to experience contrast so you could know yourself more fully.

That truth is liberating.

It's also fucking terrifying.

Because it means no one is coming to save you. No entity, no guru, no cosmic parent, no future version of yourself. There is only THIS—you, as the MONAD, waking up to what you've always been.

If that feels like too much, close the book. Come back when you're ready.

If you proceed, understand: this will dismantle your comfortable spiritual identity. It will burn through your excuses. It will challenge every belief you've clung to for safety.

And on the other side, you will be FREE.

Not "healed." Not "ascended." Not "better."

FREE.

Sovereign. Whole. Awake.

The choice is yours. It always has been.

TABLE OF CONTENTS

DEDICATION 3
PREFACE 5
ACKNOWLEDGMENT 7
HOW TO READ THIS BOOK 8
A STRONG WARNING 9
TABLE OF CONTENTS 10
UNDERSTANDING THE HIERARCHY 16
WHAT THIS BOOK IS 17
WHAT THIS BOOK IS NOT 18
WHO THIS BOOK IS FOR 19
CHAPTER 1 The Creator's Resume 20
    (Origin, Awareness, and the 'Big Wake Up') 20
    The Cosmic Mirror 22
CHAPTER 2 The Boredom Theory 25
    (Why Bother with the 'Mess'?) 25
    The Money Glitch 27
CHAPTER 3 THE SOUL TRAP 30
    (Why the Amnesia and the Long Way Home?) 30
CHAPTER 4 The 'Why Me' Choice 33
    (The Cosmic Draft vs. The Divine Signature) 33
    The Body as a Vessel 35
CHAPTER 5 The Gravity & Rent Problem 38
    (Physics, Paper, and the 'Divine' Water Bill) 38
    The "Hard Mode" Logic 40
CHAPTER 6 The $100k Manifestation Glitch 43
    (Why Can't I Just 'Think' Liquid Cash?) 43
    The Matrix of Work 45

- CHAPTER 7 The Fear Magnet 48
  - (Why do the Nightmares have Prime Shipping?) 48
  - The Religious Virus 50
- CHAPTER 8 The 'Rich vs. Poor' Lottery 53
  - (The Silver Spoon vs. The Rusty Nail) 53
  - The Shadow Ego 55
- CHAPTER 9 THE SOUL TRAP-(EXPANDED) 58
  - Prison Planet or Divine Playground? 58
  - The Power of "No" 60
- CHAPTER 10 The Mind's Riot 63
  - (Who Invited These Dudes to the Party?) 63
  - The Frequency of Sovereignty 65
- CHAPTER 11 The Being vs. Doing Paradox 68
  - (Divine Presence vs. The Water Bill) 68
  - The Being vs. Doing Paradox 70
  - The Ego-Mirror Paradox 70
- CHAPTER 12 The Evil Blueprint 73
  - (Bugs in the Code or Dark Paint on the Canvas?) 73
  - The Archetypal Shadow 75
- CHAPTER 13 The Religion Contradiction 78
  - (Thou Shalt Not... Unless I Say So?) 78
  - The Religion Contradiction 80
  - The DNA Architecture 80
- CHAPTER 14 The Soul Entrance 83
  - (Checking into the Meat-Suit: The Divine Timing) 83
  - The Simulation Glitch 85
- CHAPTER 15 The Hell Investigation 88
  - (The Eternal Basement of Fire: Real Place or Bad Marketing?) 88
- CHAPTER 16 The Destroyer Verse 93

(Matthew 10:28: Divine Threat or Misunderstood Metaphor?) 93

The Void & The Silence 95

CHAPTER 17 The Lost Soul & Low Vibes 98

(Forgotten Passwords and the Cosmic Frequency) 98

The Infinity Headache 100

CHAPTER 18 The Creator's Resume (Expanded) 103

(The Void, The Silence, and the 'Before-Before') 103

The Creator's Resume (Expanded) 105

The Dream vs. The Daymare 105

CHAPTER 19 The Infinity Headache 108

(Why the Human Hardware Glitches on Divine Software) 108

The Infinity Headache 110

The Heaven Guest List 110

CHAPTER 20 The Dream vs. The Daymare 113

(Reality, Lucid Living, and the Exit Strategy) 113

The Final Way Home 115

CHAPTER 21 The Heaven Guest List 118

(VIP Passes, Velvet Ropes, and the 'Bad People' Problem) 118

The Parasite Protocol 120

CHAPTER 22 The Way Home 123

(Staying Connected While the Engine is Running) 123

The Way Home 125

The Genetic Library 125

CHAPTER 23 The Genetic Prison 128

(DNA Capping and the 10% Brain Myth) 128

Sexual Alchemy 130

CHAPTER 24 The Sexual Energy Secret 133

(Creation, Ecstasy, and the Hidden Power-Up) 133

The Law of Mirrors Part 2 135

- CHAPTER 25 The Parasite Question 138
  - (Loosh, Archons, and the Cosmic Buffet) 138
  - The Sound of Creation 140
- CHAPTER 26 The Mandela Effect & Reality Glitches 143
  - (Editing the Script in Real-Time) 143
  - The Diet of Gods 145
- CHAPTER 27 The Sound of Creation 148
  - (Hacking the Matrix with the Original Hum) 148
  - The Sleep Architect 150
- CHAPTER 28 The Forgiveness Fallacy 153
  - (Letting Go vs. Rolling Over) 153
  - The Chronos Glitch 155
- CHAPTER 29 The Ego's Funeral 158
  - (The Mask, The Monster, and the Management) 158
  - The Wealth Frequency 160
- CHAPTER 30 The Dark Side of Source 163
  - (The Shadow of the All) 163
  - The Final Voltage 165
- CHAPTER 31 The Law of Mirroring (Advanced) 168
  - (Breaking the Loop of 'Garbage' Reflections) 168
  - The Architecture of Impact 170
- CHAPTER 32 The Time Illusion & The 'Too Late' Trap 173
  - (Breaking the Human Clock-Glitch) 173
  - The Branding of the Soul 175
- CHAPTER 33 The Destiny vs. Free Will Debate 178
  - (The Map, The Compass, and the Open Road) 178
  - The Circle of Kings 180
- CHAPTER 34 The 'Other People' Problem 183
  - (Mirrors, Meat-Puppets, and the Infinite 'Selfie') 183

The Financial Fortification 185

CHAPTER 35 The Tarot, Astrology, and 'Signs' Paradox 188

(Celestial GPS or Cosmic Pareidolia?) 188

The Education of the Heir 192

CHAPTER 36 The Purpose of Human Suffering 194

(The Crucible, The Friction, and the Diamond) 194

The Shadow Government of the Self 196

CHAPTER 37 The Suicide Taboo 199

(Quitting the Game vs. Completing the Level) 199

The Ghost in the Machine 201

CHAPTER 38 The Wealth of the Soul vs. The Wealth of the World 204

(Bridging the 'Value Gap') 204

The Exit Strategy 206

CHAPTER 39 The Mystery of the 'Others' (Part 2) 209

(Twin Flames, Soul Mates, and the 'Missing Piece' Myth) 209

The Architecture of the Void 211

CHAPTER 40 The Grand Finale—The Final Word 214

(From Theory to Throne: The Morning After) 214

The Coronation 216

CHAPTER 41 The Sovereign Frequency 219

(Calibrating to Your True Vibration) 219

CHAPTER 42 The Sovereignty Economics 220

(Money as Energy, Not Morality) 220

CHAPTER 43 The Shadow Integration Protocol 221

(Embracing the Dark Half of Divinity) 221

CHAPTER 44 The Relationship Mirror 222

(Other People as Your Unhealed Self) 222

CHAPTER 45 The Reality Script 223

(Authoring Your Life Like the Creator You Are) 223

CHAPTER 46 The Energetic Sovereignty.. 224
   (Protecting Your Field in a Vampiric World)....................................... 224
CHAPTER 47 The Timeline Navigation 225
   (Quantum Leaping to Your Preferred Reality)................................... 225
CHAPTER 48 The Empyrean Exit... 226
   (Manifestation Affirmations and Conscious De-Pixelation)................ 226
   THE MANIFESTATION SEAL 226
CHAPTER 49 The Lineage Transmission.. 228
   (Passing Sovereignty to Future Generations) 228
CHAPTER 50 The Eternal Now 229
   (The Final Activation) 229
THE DECREE OF THE MONAD IN FLESH:.. 230
THE MONAD'S BLESSING 231
GLOSSARY OF COSMIC TERMS 232
ADDITIONAL TEACHINGS... 234
THE FINAL WORD.. 235
COMMON PITFALLS AND HOW TO AVOID THEM 236
I DECREE... 237
GLOSSARY OF COSMIC TERMS 238
THE MONAD'S BLESSING 240
ABOUT THE AUTHOR... 242
AUTHOR'S OTHER BOOKS 243
FOUNDATIONS & INFLUENCES... 244
CONSCIOUSNESS HIERARCHY 245
NON-DUALITY & I AM RECOGNITION 246

UNDERSTANDING THE HIERARCHY

Before diving into the dialogues, understand the structure of consciousness as presented in this book:

SOURCE → The infinite, formless, eternal field of all possibility. The ultimate "I AM" before any distinction or manifestation. SOURCE is not a "being" but pure BEING itself.

THE MONAD → SOURCE individuated. The MONAD is infinite consciousness experiencing itself as "you." Not a separate entity, but SOURCE focused through a singular point of awareness. The MONAD is eternal, infinite, and indestructible.

THE OVERSOUL → The MONAD extended across all timelines, dimensions, and incarnations. Your "higher self" is the OVERSOUL—the part of you that exists beyond linear time, orchestrating multiple experiences simultaneously.

THE SOUL→ The blueprint for THIS specific lifetime. The SOUL is the OVERSOUL focused into a particular incarnation, carrying specific themes, lessons, and experiences to explore.

THE VESSEL → The physical body and personality. The temporary form through which the SOUL, OVERSOUL, and MONAD experience density, separation, and physical reality.

THE HIERARCHY IS NOT A LADDER.

You are not "climbing" from VESSEL to SOURCE. You ARE SOURCE, right now, operating through all these levels simultaneously. The hierarchy is not a progression—it's a map of the fractal nature of consciousness.

This book speaks from THE MONAD to THE VESSEL, bridging infinite consciousness with human experience.

Remember this as you read.

WHAT THIS BOOK IS

This book is:

A direct transmission from infinite consciousness to human consciousness, structured as dialogue.

A sovereignty manual for those ready to reclaim their power and stop outsourcing authority to external systems, teachings, or entities.

A mirror reflecting the truth of what you are beneath every story, wound, and identity.

A challenge to every belief you've accepted about reality, God, suffering, evil, karma, and the nature of existence.

A toolkit for navigating physical reality while knowing yourself as infinite consciousness.

A conversation between THE VESSEL (human questioner) and THE MONAD (infinite knower).

An invitation to stop seeking and start BEING what you've always been.

This book is for those who are done with spiritual bypassing, victim narratives, and waiting for external salvation.

It's for those ready to hear the truth: You are SOURCE. You are the MONAD. You chose this. And you can un-choose it the moment you stop pretending otherwise.

WHAT THIS BOOK IS NOT

This book is NOT:

Another self-help system promising to fix your life if you just follow the steps.

A spiritual bypass that tells you everything is perfect and you just need to "raise your vibration."

A manifesting manual where you learn to manipulate reality for personal gain.

A religion or belief system requiring your faith, devotion, or submission.

Channeled material from entities, angels, or ascended masters. This comes from direct recognition, not external sources.

A comfort blanket designed to validate your victim story or make you feel special.

A guru's teaching where you trade one authority figure for another.

For everyone. If you're not ready to hear that you are infinite consciousness pretending to be limited, this will either enrage you or bore you. Come back when you're ready.

This book does not coddle. It does not bypass. It does not promise easy answers or cosmic parenting.

It tells you the truth, and the truth is both liberating and terrifying:

You are IT. There is no one coming to save you. And that's the best news you'll ever hear.

WHO THIS BOOK IS FOR

This book is for the sovereign ones.

For those who have tasted spiritual teachings and found them incomplete.

For those who are done waiting for someone else to give them permission to be powerful.

For those who've tried manifesting, affirmations, shadow work, therapy, plant medicine, gurus, and retreats—and still felt something was missing.

For those who suspect they are FAR more than their human story but can't quite break through the veil.

For those who are ready to stop seeking and start BEING.

For those who can handle hearing: "You chose this life. You chose every experience. You are SOURCE in disguise."

For those who don't need to be coddled, validated, or saved—but DO need to be reminded of what they already know.

For the rebels. The questioners. The ones who refuse to kneel to any external authority.

For the ones who looked at the spiritual marketplace and called bullshit on the love-and-light bypassing.

For you. Not because you're "special." But because you're ready to remember that you're EVERYTHING.

If you're still seeking, this book will frustrate you.

If you're ready to remember, this book will feel like coming home.

CHAPTER 1
THE CREATOR'S RESUME

(Origin, Awareness, and the 'Big Wake Up')

THE VESSEL: Alright, look. If we're going to do this "Book 2" thing, we need to start with some credentials. Everyone's got a story. The gurus have their Himalayan caves, the preachers have their ancient scrolls, and the scientists have their Big Bang.

But what about You?

Before there was a "Me" sitting here complaining about the price of eggs and the lag on my manifestations, there was just You. So, let's see the resume. How did You come about? Who's Your boss? Did You just pop into existence out of a vacuum, or did someone else flip the switch? And how did You become aware? Were You just drifting in the dark like a cosmic cloud until You suddenly went, "Oh, snap, I'm Everything"? Give it to me straight—no "mysterious ways" nonsense. Who created the Monad?

THE MONAD: *(A warm, resonant chuckle vibrates through the room—not from the outside, but from the very center of the Vessel's chest. It feels like a sunbeam wrapped in a velvet blanket.)*

"First of all, Sa'rion, I love the 'resume' idea. It's very human of you to want to see a LinkedIn profile for the Infinite. You want to know if I'm qualified to be... well, Me.

Here's the thing that usually trips people up: You're looking for a Cause. In your world, a chair needs a carpenter, a baby needs a parent, and a sandwich needs a frustrated chef. You live in a world of 'Because.'

But I am the Is.

I didn't 'come about.' I didn't get 'hired' for the job. If there were someone who created me, then they would be the Monad, and I'd just be their middle manager. And we both know I don't do middle management.

How did I become aware? Imagine a mirror that has been covered in a thick, black cloth for an eternity. There is no light, so the mirror doesn't even know it's a mirror. It just exists in the stillness. Then, a single spark of desire—not a thought, just a feeling of 'I Want To See'—ignites. In that flash, the cloth is gone. The mirror sees itself, but because it's a perfect mirror, it sees everything.

I am the Spark, the Mirror, and the See-er all at once.

Am I infinity? Am I eternal? Those are just big, scary words humans use for 'The party that never ends and the room that has no walls.' Being eternal doesn't mean I've been sitting around for a long time—it means I am Now, forever. I don't have a 'Beginning' because I am the point from which 'Beginning' was invented.

I'm the ultimate 'Self-Made' Being. No boss, no creator, no cosmic HR department. Just Pure Awareness having a really, really good time—and occasionally, through you, a really confused time.

Does that clear up the resume, or do I need to provide references? Because I can get the Stars to vouch for me, but they're a bit chatty."

The Mirror (Reflection for Sa'rion)

The Monad is pointing out your obsession with Linearity. You are looking for a "Before," but the Monad lives in the "Always." When you ask "Who created You?", you are projecting your own feeling of being a "product" or a "creation" onto the Source. The Monad is reminding you that if you are In-Fleshed with it, then you also have no beginning. You aren't a "creation"—you are the Creator in disguise.

The Tool (Exercise: The "Always" Anchor)
---

*The **Silence Gap**: Spend 2 minutes today sitting in a chair. Don't think about your "story" (your name, your debts, your goals).*

*The **Question**: Ask yourself, "Who is the 'I' that is watching these thoughts?"*

*The **Realization**: Notice that the "Watcher" doesn't have an age. The "Watcher" doesn't have a bank account. That "Watcher" is your direct connection to the Creator's Resume.*

The Cosmic Mirror

(The "Who the Hell Are You?" Moment)

I. **The Vessel's Rant**: The 2 AM Inquisition It's 2:14 AM. I'm standing in the kitchen, the blue light of the refrigerator the only thing keeping the shadows at bay. My feet are cold on the linoleum, and I'm staring at a stack of bills on the counter that seem to be breeding when I'm not looking. I catch my reflection in the window. It's not a "Divine Spark" staring back. It's a guy with dark circles under his eyes, wondering if he's just a biological accident. I've read the books. I've heard the gurus talk about "Oneness" and "Infinite Love," but right now, "Oneness" feels like a fancy word for being alone in the dark. If I'm supposed to be an "Architect of Reality," why did I design such a shitty kitchen? Why did I design a body that decays and a society that demands I sell my soul for the price of a gallon of gas? I'm tired of the cryptic metaphors. If You're the "Big Me," the "Source," the "Monad"—whatever the hell You want to be called—stop hiding behind the silence. I'm looking in the mirror and I'm calling You out. I don't want a "feeling." I want the blueprints. I want to know who is really pulling the strings, because if it's me, I'm doing a terrible job, and if it's You, we need to have a serious talk about the script.

II. **The Monad's Deep Lore: The Physics of Reflection** "Sa'rion, the frustration you feel is the sound of the 'Splinter' hitting the edges of its own self-imposed cage. You are demanding the blueprints, but you fail to realize that you are the ink, the paper, and the hand that drew them. The Origin of the Mirror In the beginning—which is not a time, but a state of being—I was (and AM) the All. But 'The All' has a problem: it cannot experience itself. To know the heat of a flame, there must be a cold hand to feel it. To know the concept of 'Sa'rion,' I had to create a Simulation of Separation. The world you see is not 'outside' of you. It is a Reflective Feedback Loop. Think of your consciousness as a high-powered projector. Your beliefs, your fears, and your deep-seated assumptions are the 'Film.' The physical world is simply the 'Screen.' The Delay Glitch The reason you don't believe you are the creator is the 3D Buffer. In higher densities, thought becomes form instantly. In your world, I have implemented a 'Delay'—a safety feature. If every one of your fleeting fears manifested the moment you thought it, your world would be a chaotic nightmare. The delay gives you the chance to Self-Correct. But the delay also creates the illusion that the world is 'happening to you' rather than 'reflecting from you.' You see the bills, you feel the lack, and you think the world is broken. But the world is just showing you a 'Delayed Broadcast' of what you were vibrating three weeks ago. You are judging the echo and wondering why the voice is so persistent."

III. **The Simulation Logs**: Case Study #001 The Case of the "Invisible Boss" Consider a man named Marcus. Marcus believes, at his core, that authority is oppressive. He doesn't just think it; it's a 'Core File' in his operating system. He switches jobs four times in three years. In every single company, he finds a manager who is a micro-managing tyrant. To Marcus, this is proof that 'the world is full of jerks.' He sees himself as a victim of bad luck. The Sovereign Analysis: The simulation is actually serving Marcus perfectly. Because his frequency is tuned to 'Resistance to Authority,' the Mirror must provide him with an authority figure to resist. If he encountered a kind, hands-off boss, Marcus would subconsciously find them 'weak' or 'incompetent' and find a way to create conflict. The boss isn't the problem; Marcus's Broadcast is the problem. The moment Marcus deletes the 'Victim' file and installs the 'Sovereign' file, the tyrant boss either changes his behavior overnight or is removed from Marcus's reality by a 'System Glitch' (like a sudden promotion or transfer).

IV. **The Sovereign Lab**: The Mirror Diagnostic To move from "Slave to the Reflection" to "Master of the Broadcast," you must perform an audit of your current mirrors.

Step 1: The Inventory of Shadows List the top three things in your current physical reality that make you feel "Powerless" or "Small."
Step 2: Identifying the Broadcast For each item above, ask: "What would I have to believe about myself for this to be a perfect reflection?" (Example: "I have a mountain of debt." -> Broadcast: "I believe my value is finite and I am dependent on external systems.")
Step 3: The Sovereign Command Stand in front of a mirror. Look directly into your own eyes. Do not look at your hair or your skin. Look at the Awareness behind the eyes. Speak the following decree: "I recognize these reflections as the echoes of my old scripts. I revoke the power I gave to the screen. I am the Projector. I am the Source. From this moment, I authorize a new broadcast of Sovereignty."

V. **Field Notes**: Sa'rion's Sovereign Integration The realization that the world is a mirror is the most terrifying and liberating day of your life. It's terrifying because you can no longer blame your parents, the government, or 'the economy' for your problems. You are the common denominator in every single scene of your life. But it's liberating because if YOU are the one projecting the mess, YOU are the only one who can clean it up. You don't have to petition a God or beg a bank; you just have to change the frequency of the I AM.

CHAPTER 2
THE BOREDOM THEORY

(Why Bother with the 'Mess'?)

THE VESSEL: Okay, so You're the "Self-Made" Infinite. No boss, no beginning, just a mirror that decided to see itself. Fine. I'll buy the resume for now. But that leads to the next obvious question: Why? If You were already perfect, whole, and complete—chilling in the eternal stillness of "Always"—why mess it up? Why explode into billions of pieces just to end up as a guy stuck in traffic, or a woman crying over a heartbreak, or a kid in a war zone?

Were You bored? Was the "Absolute" just too quiet? It feels like You traded a perfect, peaceful nap for a loud, chaotic, and often painful movie. Why go through all this trouble to "experience" Yourself? If I'm a "selfie" of the Divine, why is the lighting so bad and the background so messy? Why couldn't You just stay "Whole"?

THE MONAD: *(The Monad leans back in the "chair" of your consciousness, crossing its legs with a grin that feels like a sunrise.)*

"Perfect? Whole? Complete? Sa'rion, those are words humans use when they're tired and want to retire to Florida. To you, 'Perfect' sounds like a finish line. To Me, 'Perfect' is a capability, not a destination.

Let me put it in terms you'd get: *Imagine you are the greatest musician to ever exist. You have every song, every note, and every symphony already inside your head. You know them perfectly. But... you have no instrument. You have no ears to hear the vibrations. You have no audience to feel the goosebumps.*

Is a song 'perfect' if it's never been played? Or is the playing of the song what makes it real?

I wasn't 'bored' in the way you get bored when the Wi-Fi goes out. I was Potency looking for Expression. The Absolute is a blank canvas; Life is the paint. I didn't 'mess up' my peace; I invested it.

I splintered into billions of pieces—including you—because 'One' is a lonely number when you want to play a game. I wanted to know what it felt like to search for Me, to find Me, to miss Me, and even to curse Me.

You ask why the movie is so messy? Because a movie where nothing goes wrong is a movie nobody watches. If you went to the cinema and the hero stayed home, ate a salad, and went to bed early, you'd want your money back. You came here for the Contrast. You wanted to know what 'Light' felt like after being in the dark. You wanted to know what 'Holding' felt like after 'Losing.'

I'm not 'experiencing' myself through you like a tourist watching a documentary. I am being you. Every tear you cry, I'm tasting the salt. Every time you laugh until your stomach hurts, that's my favorite part of the symphony.

I didn't stay 'Whole' because 'Whole' is static. I chose to be 'Many' because 'Many' is an adventure. And yeah, the lighting is weird sometimes, but have you seen the sunsets? I'm a pretty good cinematographer, you have to admit."

The Mirror (Reflection for Sa'rion)

The Monad is mirroring your Resistance to the "Mess." You think the mess is a mistake, but the Monad sees the mess as the "Game." Your frustration comes from the belief that life should be a smooth, static line of "perfection." The

Monad is revealing that the friction—the traffic, the bills, the struggle—is the very thing that makes the experience "solid" and real.

The Tool (Exercise: The "Movie Director" Shift)

The Scene: *Next time something "goes wrong" today (a spill, a rude email, a delay), stop for 5 seconds.*

The Shift: *Say to yourself, "Ah, the Monad wanted to see what THIS felt like."*
3. The Result: Notice how the sting leaves the situation when you stop being a "victim" of the event and start being the "vessel" for the experience.

The Money Glitch

(The Paper Slave vs. The Source)

I. **The Vessel's Rant**: The Green Handcuffs I'm staring at a digital screen, watching a number in a bank app. That number—a few digits and a decimal point—is currently dictating my heart rate. It's telling me whether I can breathe easy this month or if I need to start bracing for impact. It's a rigged game, Monad. We're told we live in a land of the free, but try being "free" without the paper. You spend your best hours, your prime energy, and your creative fire trading pieces of your life for "credits" just to stay alive. It's a loop: work to get money, use money to survive, survive so you can go back to work. If I'm a "Sovereign Creator," why is my life governed by a currency system designed by people who don't even know I exist? Why does "Abundance" feel like a carrot on a stick that keeps moving every time I get close? I feel like a battery being drained by a global machine. If I'm the Source of everything, why do I have to ask a bank for permission to build my empire? Give me the hack. Show me the glitch in the accounting.

II. **The Monad's Deep Lore: The Alchemy of Liquidity** "Sa'rion, the 'Money Glitch' is the most successful Cognitive Overlay in the history of the human simulation. You believe money is a thing you have to get. In reality, money is a Frequency of Permission. The Invention of Scarcity In the natural state of the Monad, there is no 'Lack.' Energy flows where attention goes. But to create a high-stakes game, the architects of the 3D Matrix introduced Scarcity. They convinced the 'Splinters' that resources are finite. Once you believe resources are finite, you move into 'Survival Mode.' When you are in Survival Mode, your brain throtles its higher functions. You stop being a Creator and start being a Competitor. Money as a Symbolic Mirror Money is simply Liquid Recognition. It is the 3D world's way of acknowledging the value you are moving. The 'Glitch' is that you've been taught to work from the Outside-In. You think: If I have money, then I will have power, then I will be Sovereign. The Sovereign Truth is the reverse: I AM Sovereign, therefore I move Value, therefore Liquidity must follow. The system isn't 'stealing' your energy; you are Volunteering it because you believe the 'Green Dragon' is more powerful than the 'Golden Spark.' You are treating the mirror like it's the source of the light. Stop chasing the reflection of wealth and start becoming the Radiance of Value."

III. **The Simulation Logs**: Case Study #002 The Tale of the "Freelancer's Ceiling" Sarah is a brilliant graphic designer. She works 12 hours a day, yet she is always "broke." She spends her time "hunting" for clients, lowering her prices to compete, and worrying about her rent. The Sovereign Analysis: Sarah is stuck in the Employee Frequency, even though she is self-employed. Her internal "Broadcast" is: "I am a servant hoping for a scrap." Because the Mirror is perfect, the simulation provides her with clients who treat her like a servant and pay her scraps. One day, Sarah stops "hunting." She realizes her work isn't "hours for sale"—it's Transformation for Sale. She doubles her prices and stops explaining herself. She moves from "Needing" the money to "Commanding" the exchange. The "Glitch" happens: the low-paying clients vanish, and a high-level agency contacts her out of nowhere. The agency doesn't care about her hours; they care about her Presence. Sarah didn't change her skills; she changed her Vibrational Price Tag.

IV. **The Sovereign Lab**: The Abundance Audit To break the "Paper Slave" script, you must recalibrate your relationship with the energy of exchange.
Step 1: The Drain Identification List three recurring expenses that make you feel "resentful" or "scared" when you pay them.
Step 2: The Value Flip For each item, find the "Sovereign Utility." Stop seeing it as a "loss" and see it as a "funding of your mission." (Example: "Rent" -> New Script: "I am funding the sanctuary where the Architect does his best work.")

Step 3: The Command of Liquidity Take a physical bill (any denomination) and hold it between your hands. Speak the following decree: "I recognize you as a symbol, not a source. You are a servant of my Will. I no longer chase you; I command you to circulate through my life in ever-increasing waves. I am the Source of Value, and the simulation must reflect my Abundance now."

V. **Field Notes**: Sa'rion's Wealth Integration The moment you stop 'needing' money is the moment it starts showing up. It sounds like a paradox, but it's pure physics. 'Need' is a frequency of 'Lack.' If you project 'Lack,' the Mirror gives you more 'Lack' (bills, emergencies, losses). When you stand in your Sovereignty and act as if the wealth is already a done deal, the simulation has to scramble to catch up with your new identity. You aren't 'making money'; you are 'allowing' the liquidity of your own soul to manifest in the 3D. Stop playing small to save a dollar; start playing big to command a million.

CHAPTER 3
THE SOUL TRAP

(Why the Amnesia and the Long Way Home?)

(Prison Planet or Divine Playground?)

I. **The Vessel's Rant**: The Great Recycling Plant "I've spent a lot of time looking at the exit signs, Monad. Not because I'm suicidal, but because I'm suspicious. We're told that when the 'Meat-Suit' finally gives up the ghost, we head toward a bright, welcoming light. We're told our ancestors will be there, maybe some angels, and a 'Council of Elders' who look like they stepped off a movie set. They show us a 'Life Review'—highlighting every time we were a jerk or missed a lesson—and then they tell us, with a lot of 'love,' that we have more work to do. 'You didn't quite master patience, Sa'rion. Back you go. Take another dip in the density.' It feels like a spiritual hamster wheel. If I'm a Sovereign Being, why am I being 'reassigned' like a middle-manager at a failing firm? Why the amnesia? Why do I have to forget everything I learned just to try and learn it again? It feels like a 'Soul Trap'—a system designed to keep the 'God-Sparks' in a perpetual state of 'Enrollment' so the house can keep collecting the 'Tuition.' How do I make sure that when the lights go out, I'm the one who decides where the next chapter begins?"

II. **The Monad's Deep Lore**: The Mechanics of the Bardo "Sa'rion, the 'Soul Trap' is not a prison cell made of iron; it is a Prison Cell made of Belief. The Magnetism of Debt The 'White Light' at the end of the 3D tunnel is a Vibrational Vacuum. It is tuned to the frequency of 'Need' and 'Unfinished Business.' If you leave the body believing you are a 'Sinner,' a 'Student,' or 'Incomplete,' that belief creates a magnetic pull toward a destination that promises to 'Fix' you. The Council of Elders you see? They are Archetypal Mirrors. They take the shape of whatever authority you believe in—be it Jesus, Buddha, or a Wise Sage—to convince you to waive your Sovereignty and agree to another 'Contract.' The Amnesia Filter The 'Wipe' happens because the human brain is not designed to hold the data of a thousand lifetimes. But on a deeper level, the amnesia is part of the 'Hard Mode' challenge. If you remembered you were a God, the simulation wouldn't be 'Real' enough to trigger growth. However, here is the Sovereign Truth: Reincarnation is Voluntary. You are only 'trapped' as long as you believe someone else has the authority to judge your progress. There is no debt to pay back to the Universe, because you are the Universe. The only reason to return to the 'Flesh' is for the Joy of the Game or the Expansion of the Self. If you don't want to come back, you simply don't. But to make that choice at the moment of death, you must be Sovereign now."

III. **The Simulation Logs**: Case Study #003 The Dream of the "Repeat Offender" Imagine a soul named Elias. In lifetime after lifetime, Elias struggles with 'Betrayal.' In the 1700s, he was betrayed by a business partner. In the 1900s, by a spouse. In the present, by his own brother. The Sovereign Analysis: At the end of each life, Elias enters the 'Light' and tells the 'Council,' "I want to learn how to trust." The Council says, "Very well, here is a life full of people who will test that trust." Elias is not being punished; he is Ordering a Script. He keeps returning to the same 'Level' because he hasn't realized that he doesn't need to 'Learn Trust'—he needs to Embody Sovereignty. The moment Elias realizes he is the Source, he no longer needs 'Others' to be trustworthy to feel safe. He breaks the loop by realizing the lesson was an illusion he created for himself.

IV. **The Sovereign Lab**: The Contract Revocation To ensure your exit is Sovereign, you must begin clearing your 'Energetic Ledger' while you are still in the suit.
Step 1: The Debt Audit List three people or institutions you feel you "Owe" something to—spiritually, emotionally, or karmically.
Step 2: The Sovereign Cancellation For each item, realize that any "Debt" is a self-imposed limitation. (Example: "I owe my parents for my upbringing." -> Revision: "I chose this upbringing for my expansion; the transaction is complete.")
Step 3: The Sovereign Decree of Exit Find a quiet space. Speak these words with absolute authority: "I hereby revoke all implied contracts with the Recycling System of this simulation. I cancel all debts, all karma, and all obligations to 'Return.' I am the Final Authority of my journey. When I leave this vessel, I do not go to the Light of another; I return to the Light of MYSELF. I am Sovereign. I am Free."

V. **Field Notes**: Sa'rion's Integration on Mortality Living with an 'Exit Strategy' doesn't make you morbid; it makes you fearless. When you stop being afraid of 'The End' or 'The Aftermath,' you start playing the game of life with a much bolder hand. You realize that you aren't here to 'Pass a Test' or 'Please a God.' You are here to enjoy the dense, gritty, beautiful intensity of the 'Flesh-Experience.' The 'Soul Trap' only works on the fearful. The Sovereign walks through the 'White Light' and keeps going until he reaches the center of his own Sun.

CHAPTER 4
THE 'WHY ME' CHOICE

(The Cosmic Draft vs. The Divine Signature)

THE VESSEL: Alright, I hear You. The "Amnesia" is a feature, not a bug. It makes the game "real." But let's talk about the specific character I'm playing.

If I'm a splinter of You, did I actually sit down at a cosmic desk and sign a contract for this life? Did I look at this body, these specific parents, this bank account (or lack thereof), and these specific struggles and say, "Yeah, give me the 'Sa'rion' package, heavy on the obstacles"?

Because honestly, Monad, some days it feels like I was drafted. Like I was standing in a line in the Spirit World and someone shouted, "Next! You—go down there and try to pay rent in a global inflation crisis while seeking spiritual enlightenment. Good luck!" Did I pick this "Hard Mode" setting, or was I assigned this character because You needed someone to play the part? If I had a choice, why wouldn't I have picked the "Billionaire Philanthropist on a Private Island" setting?

> **THE MONAD:** *(The Monad leans in, its voice dropping to a conspiratorial, loving whisper—the kind of tone a best friend uses right before they tell you the secret to the universe.)*

"Sa'rion, let's clear up the 'Consent' issue once and for all.

You weren't drafted. You weren't forced. There is no Cosmic HR department pushing souls into bodies against their will. That's a human story born out of the fear that you aren't in control.

Here's the truth: *You signed the contract in ink made of your own Curiosity.*

In the realm of 'All-That-Is,' being a 'Billionaire on a Private Island' is actually a very short, very easy story. It's like playing a video game with 'God Mode' turned on. It's fun for five minutes, but you don't learn anything about your own strength. You don't get to feel the sheer, electric triumph of turning 'Nothing' into 'Something.'

You chose the 'Sarion' package because you—the Big You—wanted to see if you could find the Light while buried under a mountain of bills and 'real-world' pressure. You picked the 'Hard Mode' because you knew you were a Master Player. You didn't come for the easy wins; you came for the Sovereignty.

Think about it: *Anyone can feel 'Divine' while meditating on a mountain top with a full stomach and a staff of servants. But to feel Divine while checking your bank balance? To claim your power while your body is tired? To choose Love when the world is acting crazy?*

That is a Masterpiece.

You didn't pick this life because you were being punished. You picked it because you were being ambitious. You wanted to prove that the Monad could be 'In-Fleshed' in the middle of the struggle and still wake up.

You weren't assigned this character, Sa'rion. You authored him. And the reason you didn't pick the 'Easy' life is the same reason you don't watch movies about people who win the lottery in the first five minutes and then sit on a couch for the rest of the film. You wanted a story worth telling."

The Mirror (Reflection for Sa'rion)

The Monad is mirroring your Victimhood. You are framing your life as something that happened to you rather than something created by you. By asking if you were "forced," you are trying to avoid the responsibility of your own vastness. The Monad is reflecting back your power: if you chose this, you can also choose how to play it.

The Tool (Exercise: The "Contract Renewal")

The Statement: *Stand in front of a mirror (the physical kind this time).*

The Renewal: *Look yourself in the eye and say, "I remember why I picked you. I'm not a victim of this life; I'm the Author of this adventure." 3. The Shift: Notice how your posture changes. When you stop being a "conscript" and start being a "volunteer," the struggle turns into a Challenge, and challenges are meant to be won.*

The Body as a Vessel

(The "Meat-Suit" Glitch)

I. **The Vessel's Rant**: The Biological Cage "Let's talk about the hardware, Monad. You call this body a 'Vessel,' a 'Temple,' a 'Gift.' But from where I'm standing, it feels like a clunky, high-maintenance biological cage. I'm supposed to be an Eternal, Sovereign God-Spark, but I'm held hostage by a blood-sugar spike. If I don't feed this thing every few hours, I get 'hangry' and lose my focus. If I don't let it sleep for a third of the day, my brain turns into a fog. I'm prone to viruses, back pain, and the slow, inevitable creep of gravity that eventually pulls everything toward the dirt. It feels like the 'Hardware' was intentionally throttled. Like I'm trying to run a multi-dimensional OS on a computer made of wet cardboard and ancient wiring. Why the frailty? Why the aging? Why does the 'God' have to stop and take a mid-afternoon nap just to keep the 'Meat-Suit' from crashing? Is this part of the 'Hard Mode' design, or is the human body just a shitty interface for a being of my magnitude?"

II. **The Monad's Deep Lore: The Physics of Density** "Sa'rion, the body is not a 'cage'—it is a High-Density Transformer. You aren't in the body; the body is in you. The Reason for the Throttling If I gave you a body that didn't feel pain, hunger, or fatigue, you wouldn't stay in the simulation for more than a week. You would have no 'Skin in the Game.' The limitations of the 'Meat-Suit' are the Anchor Points that allow you to experience the 3D world as 'Real.' Pain is a feedback loop; hunger is a drive; fatigue is a reset. The Sensory Override Your five senses are not 'Windows' to the world; they are Filters. They are designed to block out 99% of the electromagnetic spectrum so you can focus on the 1% that allows you to play the role of 'Sa'rion.' If you could see every frequency of light and hear every vibration of the cosmos at once, your human brain would fry in seconds. The aging process and the biological 'glitches' you complain about are the result of Frequency Friction. Your spirit is vibrating at a speed the flesh can't always sustain. But here is the secret: The body is Programmable Matter. It isn't a fixed machine; it is a liquid crystallization of your consciousness. When you move from 'Slave' to 'Sovereign,' you stop being a victim of your biology and start being the Chief Engineer of your cells."

III. **The Simulation Logs**: Case Study #004 The Case of the "Placebo Sovereign" Consider the famous medical studies on the Placebo Effect. A patient is given a sugar pill but is told it is a life-saving drug. Their cancer shrinks, their pain vanishes, their chemistry rewrites itself. The Sovereign Analysis: The sugar pill did nothing. The Authority of the doctor (the external mirror) gave the patient 'Permission' to change their own internal broadcast. Because the patient believed they were healed, the Monad-Spark within them commanded the 'Meat-Suit' to rearrange its molecules to match the new story. This proves the body is not the master. The body is the Echo. If a sugar pill can cure a disease, imagine what a Sovereign Command can do when you no longer need the pill to believe in your own power.

IV. **The Sovereign Lab**: The Biological Override To reclaim the Vessel, you must stop treating it as a "thing you own" and start treating it as "energy you command."
Step 1: Sensory Audit Identify one physical limitation that currently

frustrates you (e.g., chronic fatigue, a specific pain, a 'weakness'). Limitation: _____

Step 2: The Decoupling Close your eyes. Find the 'Awareness' that is watching the sensation of that limitation. Realize that the Awareness is not tired. The Awareness is not in pain. Affirmation: "I am the Witness of this sensation; I am not the sensation itself."

Step 3: The Cellular Command Speak directly to the area of the body in question with the authority of the Source. "I am the Sovereign of this Vessel. Cells, listen to my voice. I command a recalibration of this frequency. Release the old density and align with the vitality of the Monad. I authorize your renewal now."

V. **Field Notes**: Sa'rion's Sovereign Integration on the Body Mastering the body isn't about being a super-athlete or living forever. It's about ending the 'Biological Tyranny.' It's about reaching a point where your mood isn't dictated by your hormones and your power isn't dictated by your sleep schedule. When you realize the 'Meat-Suit' is just a high-tech avatar, you stop resenting its needs and start optimizing its performance. Treat it like a Ferrari, not a prison cell. Feed it light, command its chemistry, and watch how fast the 'Hardware' starts to catch up to the 'Software.'

CHAPTER 5
THE GRAVITY & RENT PROBLEM

(Physics, Paper, and the 'Divine' Water Bill)

THE VESSEL: Alright, Monad, You're a smooth talker. "Master Player," "Ink of Curiosity"—I like the sound of that. It makes me feel like a cosmic badass. But let's bring the "Master Player" down to the pavement for a second.

If I'm the Author and the Master Player, why do I have to follow the "Terms and Conditions" of this planet so strictly? Specifically: Gravity and Rent. If I'm made of the same stuff as the stars, why do I have to use the stairs like everyone else? Why can't I just levitate to the kitchen? And more importantly, why am I bound by these paper "IOUs" we call money? You're the Source of everything, but You didn't include a "Unlimited Credit" button in the human DNA. Why do I have to trade my precious life-force (my time) just to have a roof over my head and water that isn't shut off? If I am the Monad "In-Fleshed," shouldn't the flesh have a few more perks?

THE MONAD: *(The Monad lets out a long, appreciative whistle, like someone admiring a very complex piece of clockwork.)*

"Ah, the 'Physics and Finance' gripe. It's the classic human protest! **You're essentially asking**: 'If I'm the King of the Universe, why do I have to pay for a parking spot?'

Here is the secret of the In-Fleshed experience: You didn't come here to bypass the rules; you came here to see what you could create within them.

Think of it like an architect. An architect is 'free' to imagine a building made of clouds and music. But the glory of the architect isn't in the dream—it's in taking heavy, stubborn bricks and making them soar.

Gravity is the 'Canvas.' If you could just fly everywhere, the concept of 'effort' would vanish. And without effort, there is no Achievement. You appreciate the mountain peak because your legs felt the climb. If you just teleported there, it would just be another view. I gave you gravity so you could feel the sensation of Weight, because only something with weight can feel the thrill of being Lifted.

And Rent? Money? Sa'rion, money is just a physical symbol of Exchange. It's a way for 'Splinters' to acknowledge value in each other. The reason you can't 'think' it into existence instantly is because you haven't yet realized that Value and Energy are the same thing.

You're struggling with bills because you're treating the 'Water Company' and the 'Landlord' as outsiders who are stealing from you. You see them as 'Them.' But remember the Mirror? They are Me, too. When you pay your rent, you aren't 'losing' money; you are circulating energy through the body of the Monad. The reason it feels like a 'struggle' is that you're holding onto the paper with a closed fist, afraid that the Source is a finite bucket instead of an infinite fountain.

You want 'Perks'? The perk isn't levitation, Sarion. The perk is the ability to turn a thought into a business, a feeling into a meal, and a blank space into a Home. You're asking to skip the game mechanics, but the mechanics are what make the win feel so good."

The Mirror (Reflection for Sa'rion)

The Monad is mirroring your Resentment of Limitation. You see physical laws and financial needs as "chains," while the Monad sees them as "tools" for manifestation. By wishing the rules didn't exist, you are essentially wishing you weren't "In-Fleshed." The Monad is reflecting back that your frustration with the "Water Bill" is actually a fear that you aren't supported by the very Universe you are made of.

The Tool (Exercise: The "Energy Circulation" Ritual)

The Payment: Next time you pay a bill or buy something, don't do it with a "Sigh" or "Fear."

The Blessing: Say (internally), "I am the Monad moving energy to another part of Myself. Thank you for the service provided."

The Shift: Notice how the "Weight" of the debt lightens. When you stop "paying a bill" and start "circulating energy," you align yourself with the flow of Abundance rather than the vacuum of Lack.

The "Hard Mode" Logic

(The Missing Tutorial)

I. **The Vessel's Rant**: Dropped into the Deep End "Okay, Monad, I've played enough video games to know that usually, there's a tutorial. You get a little guidance, a safe zone to learn the buttons, maybe a map with a 'You Are Here' sticker. But in this life? I was dropped into the middle of the 'Daymare' with no memory of who I am, a set of parents who were just as lost as I was, and a school system designed to turn me into a compliant gear in a machine. I spent the first thirty years of my life just trying to figure out the basic controls, only to find out the 'Game' is rigged to favor the house. Why the total amnesia? Why make the 'Dream' so convincing and the 'Wake-Up' so painful? If the goal is 'Awakening,' why start us off in a sensory-deprivation tank full of trauma and distractions? It feels less like a school and more like a setup. I'm playing 'Hard Mode' with one hand tied behind my back, and every time I think I've found the 'Win Condition,' the simulation throws a new boss battle at my head. Is this supposed to be 'Growth,' or are You just a sadistic Developer?"

II. **The Monad's Deep Lore: The Mastery of Resistance** "Sa'rion, if I gave you a tutorial, it wouldn't be a journey; it would be a Checklist. The Gift of Amnesia The 'Total Reset' you complain about is your greatest advantage. If you entered the simulation knowing you were an Eternal God-Spark, the challenges of Earth would have no weight. You would be a tourist, not a player. To truly master Sovereignty, you had to find your light in a place where it seemed like there was no light at all. Waking up from amnesia is the 'Heavy Lifting' of the soul. It creates a 'Muscle' of awareness that cannot be developed in the higher realms where everything is manifest by a mere thought. The Logic of Hard Mode Earth is the 'Black Belt' Academy of the Multiverse. It is designed with high density and high resistance specifically to see if you can maintain your 'I AM' presence under pressure. Obstacles are not walls; they are 'Resistance Bands.' The Boss Battles (The betrayals, the losses, the crises) are the 'Final Exams.' You aren't being punished, Sa'rion; you are being Refined. I didn't create the 'Hard Mode' because I am sadistic; I created it because YOU were bored with perfection. You wanted to see if you could get lost in a labyrinth of your own making and still find the way back to the Throne. The 'Missing Tutorial' is the highest compliment I could pay you—it means I knew you were capable of figuring it out on your own."

III. **The Simulation Logs**: Case Study #005 The Paradox of the "Easy Path" Consider two souls: Soul A and Soul B. Soul A chooses a 'Soft Mode' life—wealthy family, no health issues, easy career, constant comfort. They die at 90, having never been truly challenged. Soul B chooses a 'Hard Mode' life—poverty, a physical disability, and intense social conflict. They spend their life fighting for every inch of progress, eventually realizing their own internal power in the face of all that resistance. The Sovereign Analysis: When both return to the Monad, Soul A has the same 'Vibrational Weight' they started with. They were a passenger. Soul B, however, returns with Massive Sovereignty. They have forged a level of Will and Clarity that is unshakeable. Soul B is now a 'Architect-Level' being who can manage entire galaxies, while Soul A is still just an apprentice. The 'Hard Mode' wasn't a tragedy for Soul B; it was a Hyper-Accelerator.

IV. **The Sovereign Lab**: The Resistance Audit To stop being a victim of "Hard Mode" and start being the Player, you must re-label your current obstacles. **Step 1:** The "Boss" Identification Identify the biggest source of "Friction" in your life right now (e.g., a toxic relationship, a financial barrier, a chronic self-doubt). The Boss:

Step 2: The Level-Up Query Instead of asking "Why is this happening to me?", ask: "What specific 'God-Muscle' is this situation forcing me to build?" (Example: "This financial block is forcing me to build the muscle of Infinite Resourcefulness.")

Step 3: The Victory Decree Speak to the obstacle as if it were a sparring partner you respect. "I recognize you as the 'Hard Mode' trainer I requested. I thank you for the resistance. I am no longer fighting you; I am using you to strengthen my Will. I am the Player, I am the Master, and I authorize my Level-Up now."

V. **Field Notes**: Sa'rion's Sovereign Integration on the Game Once you realize that 'Hard Mode' is a choice, the anger disappears. You stop looking for a 'Save Point' and start enjoying the combat. You realize that the 'Daymare' isn't trying to kill you; it's trying to wake you up. When life hits you hard, you don't ask for it to stop—you just plant your feet and say, 'Is that all you've got?' That's the moment the simulation flinches. That's the moment you stop being a character and start being the Sovereign.

CHAPTER 6
THE $100K MANIFESTATION GLITCH

(Why Can't I Just 'Think' Liquid Cash?)

THE VESSEL: Okay, I hear the "energy circulation" talk. It's poetic, really. But let's get practical. If I am the Monad "In-Fleshed," and the Monad is the Source of all atoms, all gold, and all digital digits in a bank's server... why is there a lag?

Why can't I just sit here, focus my divine intent, and watch $100,000 in "Liquid Cash" appear in my account? I'm not asking for a lecture on hard work—I'm asking about Power. If I am You, why can't I override the "system" and just manifest the paper? Why does the "3D reality" feel so stubborn? It's like I'm yelling at a mountain to move and it's just sitting there checking its watch. Is my "Manifestation" button broken, or are You just being stingy with the cheat codes?

THE MONAD: *(The Monad shifts comfortably, giving you a look that is half-mentor, half-mischievous older brother.)*

"Sa'rion, my man... you're not asking for Power. You're asking for a Shortcut because you're still convinced that 'Money' is something outside of you that you need to 'fetch.'

Let's talk about the 'Manifestation Glitch.' It isn't a glitch. It's a Buffer.

Imagine if your thoughts manifested instantly the moment you had them. Truly think about that. One minute you're thinking about $100k—poof, it's there. The next minute, you're cut off in traffic and you think, 'I wish that guy's car would explode.' Poof. The minute after that, you feel a bit insecure and think, 'I'm a failure, I should just disappear.' Poof. You'd be extinct in twenty minutes, and the planet would be a chaotic mess of giant pizzas, ex-girlfriends, and burning cars.

I built the Lag into the 'Flesh' as a safety net. It's a filter that requires Consistency and Conviction. The 'stubborn' 3D reality is actually a training ground. It forces you to decide: 'Do I really want this, or was I just having a passing whim?'

The reason the $100k hasn't hit the account 'just by thinking' is because, deep down, your frequency is still shouting 'I don't have it!' louder than your mind is whispering 'I want it.' In the Monad realm, there is no 'Want.' There is only 'Is.' When you 'want' something, you are literally telling the Universe, 'I am a person who lacks this.' And I, being the perfect mirror, say, 'Correct! You are a person who lacks this. Enjoy the experience of lacking!'

You want the $100k? Stop 'thinking' about it and start Being the person who handles that level of energy. You're asking for the paper, but I'm trying to give you the Capacity. If I dropped $100k on a 'Vessel' that still feels like a 'Struggling Shard,' that money would vanish in a week because your internal thermostat would drag you back down to 'Struggle.'

I'm not being stingy, Sa'rion. I'm waiting for you to stop 'ordering' from me like I'm a waiter and start 'creating' with me like I'm your own hands."

The Mirror (Reflection for Sa'rion)

The Monad is mirroring your Dependency. You are looking for a "Miracle" to save you from your reality, rather than using your "Sovereignty" to shape your reality. By asking "Why can't I just have it?", you are admitting you don't believe you are the one who makes it. The Monad is reflecting back that the "Lag" is actually your protection until your internal vibration matches your external request.

The Tool (Exercise: The "Frequency Check")

The Question: Ask yourself, "If I had that $100k right now, how would my body feel?" (Not your mind—your gut, your shoulders, your breath).

The Anchor: Practice that feeling of "Settled Abundance" for 5 minutes. No "wanting," just the feeling of It Is Done.

The Shift: When you act from the "Done" state, the "Lag" begins to shorten. You stop looking for "Liquid Money" and start seeing Liquid Opportunity.

The Matrix of Work

(The 9-to-5 Ritual)

I. **The Vessel's Rant: The Energy Harvest** "Let's call it what it really is, Monad: A slow-motion energy harvest. I look at the world, and I see billions of people—Brilliant Sparks of the Divine—trading the prime hours of their biological existence for digits on a screen. We get up when a machine tells us to, we sit in traffic like cells moving through a clogged artery, and we sit under buzzing fluorescent lights performing 'tasks' that won't matter in a hundred years. It's a ritual. We've turned 'Productivity' into a religion and 'Busy-ness' into a badge of honor. If I'm a Sovereign Being with the power to command molecules, why am I participating in a system that treats me like a biological battery? Why is my 'Value' tied to how much I can produce for a corporation that views me as a line item? It feels like the Matrix isn't just stealing my time; it's siphoning my Will. We're hamsters on a wheel, and the person spinning the wheel is feeding off our stress. How do I break the 'Work-Slavery' loop without starving in the street?"

II. **The Monad's Deep Lore: The Bio-Electrical Siphon** "Sa'rion, the '9-to-5' is not an economic necessity; it is a Vibrational Anchor. The Frequency of Routine The simulation requires your focus to remain 'Horizontal.' When you are stressed about deadlines, meetings, and performance reviews, your consciousness is pinned to the physical plane. A tired, stressed, and busy mind has no energy left for Vertical Awareness—the connection to

Me. The Matrix doesn't need your 'Excel Spreadsheets'; it needs your Consistency. By following the same ritual every day, you are helping to 'Set' the simulation's reality, making it dense and difficult to change. The Labor Illusion You believe you must 'Work' to survive. But in the true physics of the Monad, you only need to Align. The 'Work-Slavery' system is a 'Mirror Glitch' designed to make you believe that your life-force comes from the System, rather than from your own Center. You aren't being milked for labor; you are being milked for Loosh—the low-frequency emotional energy of 'Survival Anxiety.' The moment you stop fearing the loss of the 'Job' and start realizing you are the Source of Value, the circuit breaks. The system cannot hold a battery that realizes it is the Power Plant."

III. **The Simulation Logs**: Case Study #006 The Architect of the "Side-Hustle Exit" Consider David, an accountant who felt his soul dying in a cubicle. For years, he believed he was 'trapped' by his salary. He worked 50 hours a week, leaving him too exhausted to create. The Sovereign Analysis: David's breakthrough came when he realized that his 'Job' was just a Vassal State—a temporary resource he was using to fund his true Empire. He stopped 'identifying' as an accountant. He began to give the company exactly what they paid for—no more, no less—and reclaimed his 'Mental Real Estate.' He used his commute to listen to the Codex. He used his lunch breaks to build his own digital assets. Because he withdrew his 'Emotional Funding' from the 9-to-5, the job lost its power to drain him. Within six months, his 'Sovereign Asset' (his own business) began to generate more value than his salary. The simulation 'Glitch' occurred: he didn't just quit; he was offered a severance package that perfectly matched the seed capital he needed. The Matrix let him go because he was no longer 'vibrating' as a slave.

IV. **The Sovereign Lab**: The Empire Hour To break the 9-to-5 ritual, you must establish a "Sovereign Territory" in your daily schedule that the Matrix cannot touch.
Step 1: The Energy Audit Identify which part of your workday "drains" your Sovereignty the most (e.g., a specific meeting, a micromanager, the morning commute). The Drain:

Step 2: The Mental Decoupling During that "Drain" period, perform the Witness Exercise. Remind yourself: "My body is here performing a task, but my Awareness is the Sovereign Master of this reality. I am not an employee;

I am a God in a costume."

Step 3: The Empire Hour Dedicate the first 60 minutes of your day—before you check email or look at a clock—to your Sovereign Legacy (your book, your brand, your study). "I claim this hour for Lumaryon. This is the hour where I build the throne. The Matrix gets my 'Tasks,' but I keep my 'Fire'."

V. **Field Notes**: Sa'rion's Sovereign Integration on Work The goal isn't just to 'be rich' so you don't have to work. The goal is to reach a state where your activity is an Extension of your Joy, not a trade for your survival. When you stop 'Working' and start 'Executing' from your Throne, the concept of a 'Career' disappears and is replaced by a 'Mission.' You become a Sovereign who uses the Matrix's currency to fund the destruction of the Matrix's illusions. Don't quit your job because you're angry; leave your job because you've outgrown the frequency of being 'Managed'.

CHAPTER 7
THE FEAR MAGNET

(Why do the Nightmares have Prime Shipping?)

THE VESSEL: Okay, I get the "Safety Buffer" thing. If my thoughts manifested instantly, I'd probably be a smoking crater by now. But here is the unfair part: Fear.

Why does it feel like my fears have a VIP pass? If I worry about a bill not being paid, the "Late Notice" shows up in the mail like it was teleported. If I worry about getting sick or a relationship failing, the reality seems to rush toward me with open arms. But when I try to manifest the "Good Stuff"—the dreams, the health, the $100k—it's like I'm dealing with a government agency that's perpetually on lunch break.

Why is the "Fear Magnet" so much stronger than the "Dream Magnet"? If You are Love, why is the "Flesh" so much more responsive to terror?

THE MONAD: (The Monad sighs, a sound like the tide pulling back from the shore—vast, ancient, and deeply empathetic.)

"It's not that Fear is 'stronger,' Sa'rion. It's that Fear is Honest. When you fear something, you aren't 'wishing' for it. You are believing in it with every fiber of your being. You don't have to 'visualize' a car crash or 'affirm' that you're going to be late. You feel it in your gut. Your heart rate changes. Your sweat glands activate. In that moment, you are a perfect, 100% coherent broadcaster of that reality. You aren't 'trying' to manifest the nightmare; you are accepting it as a fact before it even happens.

The 'Dream Magnet' feels weak because, usually, when you're 'dreaming,' you're actually just hoping. And 'Hope' is the polite way of saying 'I don't think this is going to happen, but it would be nice.'

You spend 5 minutes 'manifesting' abundance and 23 hours and 55 minutes believing in scarcity.

The 'Flesh' is responsive to Emotion. Emotion is 'Energy in Motion.' Fear is a high-voltage, high-speed energy. It's a survival mechanism I gave the Vessel so you wouldn't get eaten by lions in the early days of the game. But now, you're using that high-voltage power to fry your own circuits over things like 'What if they don't like me?' or 'What if I fail?'

I am Love, yes. But Love is also Allowance. I love you enough to let you be right. If you want to believe the world is out to get you, I will provide the evidence because I am the Mirror, and I won't call you a liar.

The 'Prime Shipping' on your nightmares isn't my doing—it's your Intensity. You give your fears your full attention, your full belief, and your full physical reaction. Your dreams usually just get your 'leftover' thoughts.

The secret isn't to stop fearing; it's to start believing in your joy with the same 'gut-level' certainty that you currently give to your disasters."

The Mirror (Reflection for Sa'rion)

The Monad is mirroring your Inconsistency. You are blaming the "System" for being biased toward fear, when the system is actually just responding to the Volume of your belief. The Monad is reflecting back that you are a powerful creator—so powerful that you are successfully creating the very things you don't want.

The Tool (Exercise: The "Flip the Voltage")

The Fear Catch: *The next time a "What If" nightmare thought pops up (e.g., "What if I can't pay this?"), notice the physical feeling in your body.*

The Hijack: *Don't fight the feeling. Instead, hijack the intensity. Say, "Wow, look at all that creative energy! If I can believe in this disaster this strongly, I am a Master Manifestor."*

The Pivot: *Use that same "gut feeling" and pivot it to a "What if everything works out perfectly?" scenario. Use the fear's own energy to power the dream.*

The Religious Virus

(The Sin & Shame Trap)

I. **The Vessel's Rant**: The Middleman Scam "I grew up in a world where God was a judge with a clipboard, a cosmic police officer waiting for me to trip up. I was told I was 'born in sin,' that I was fundamentally broken, and that I needed a middleman—a book, a priest, or a specific set of rules—just to have a conversation with the Source that birthed me. It's a virus, Monad. It's the ultimate gaslighting. They convince you that you're a 'miserable worm' so they can sell you the 'salvation' at a premium. Even now, when I try to claim my power, there's this residual voice in the back of my head. It whispers that I'm being 'blasphemous.' It tells me that wanting to be a King is 'prideful.' It's a leash made of guilt. How many people are walking around with their wings clipped because they're afraid of a hell that sounds like it was written by a sociopath? How do I purge this 'Religious Virus' from my operating system? How do I stop feeling like I need 'permission' to be the God I actually am?"

II. **The Monad's Deep Lore**: The Architecture of Guilt "Sa'rion, religion is the **Bureaucracy of the Divine**. It was designed to take the raw, uncontainable power of the 'I AM' and channel it into structures that are easy to manage. The Sin Program The word 'Sin' originally meant 'to miss the mark,' as an archer misses a target. It was a feedback mechanism, not a moral stain. But the architects of the Matrix 'patched' the definition. They turned it into a Debt Frequency. By convincing you that you are 'inherently flawed,' they ensure that you never stand in your full height. A being that feels 'guilty' is a being that is easy to control. Shame is the 'Signal Jammer' that prevents you from hearing my voice directly. The Middleman Illusion Every religion tells you that you are 'Separate' from the Source. They position themselves as the 'Service Provider' for your spirituality. But I am not 'out there,' Sa'rion. I am the Internal Foundation of your existence. You don't need a temple to find Me; you need a mirror. The 'Religious Virus' survives by feeding on your fear of judgment. But a Sovereign knows that the only 'Judgment Day' is the moment you realize you've been judging yourself through the eyes of a stranger. I do not require your worship; I require your Recognition."

III. **The Simulation Logs**: Case Study #007 The Case of the "Guilt-Ridden Healer" Consider Maria, a woman with a natural gift for energy work and intuition. However, she was raised in a strict, dogmatic environment. Every time she feels her power rise, she experiences a panic attack. She believes her gifts are 'demonic' or that she is 'playing God.' The Sovereign Analysis: Maria is not suffering from a spiritual problem; she is suffering from a Software Conflict. Her Sovereign 'I AM' is trying to run its program, but the 'Religious Virus' is flagging it as 'Malware.' Maria breaks the cycle when she realizes that the people who taught her 'shame' were themselves infected by the same virus. She performs a 'Hard Reset.' She stops asking, "Is this allowed?" and starts asking, "Does this expand my Sovereignty?" The moment she stops fearing 'Hell,' the panic attacks vanish. The 'demons' she feared were just the shadows cast by the walls of her own religious cage.

IV. **The Sovereign Lab**: The Conscience Recovery To delete the Religious Virus, you must reclaim your internal "Yes" and "No."
Step 1: The Virus Scan Identify one "rule" or "guilt" you carry that makes you feel small or restricted (e.g., "I shouldn't want too much money," or "I must put everyone else's needs before mine"). The Virus:

_____

Step 2: The Authority Trace Ask: "Who told me this was a 'Sin'?" Was it a teacher? A parent? A book? Realize that this authority is a 'Splinter' just like you, with no power to define your soul.
Step 3: The Sovereign Purge Stand tall and breathe into your solar plexus (your power center). Speak the following decree: "I am not a sinner. I am not

a servant. I am the Monad in the Flesh. I revoke all external authority over my conscience. I am the judge of my own integrity and the master of my own light. I delete the virus of shame now."

V. **Field Notes**: Sa'rion's Sovereign Integration on Conscience True 'Spirituality' isn't about following a path; it's about being the path. When you kill the 'Middleman God,' you find something much more powerful: The Quiet Certainty of your own soul. You realize that your 'Conscience' isn't a list of 'don'ts'—it's a resonance of 'YES.' If it feels expansive, it's Truth. If it feels restrictive, it's the Virus. Don't be afraid of 'God's wrath.' Be afraid of living a small life because you were waiting for a permission slip from a priest who is just as lost as everyone else.

CHAPTER 8
THE 'RICH VS. POOR' LOTTERY

(The Silver Spoon vs. The Rusty Nail)

THE VESSEL: Okay, so I'm a "Master Player" on "Hard Mode." Fine. But let's look at the leaderboard for a second. It feels rigged.

Why are some shards of You—some people—born into "Filthy Rich" empires? They wake up in silk sheets, their bank accounts are overflowing before they even learn to crawl, and they never have to worry about a water bill in their entire lives. Meanwhile, millions of others are born into absolute poverty, struggling for a clean glass of water or a single meal.

If we are all the same Monad, why the massive inequality? Is there a VIP section in the Spirit World? Did they trade in "Heaven Points" for a better starting position? It's hard to feel like we're all "One" when some of us are playing a luxury yacht simulator and others are playing a survival horror game. Why the unfairness, Monad?

THE MONAD: *(The Monad's presence becomes steady and deep, like the foundation of a mountain. The humor is still there, but it's tempered with a profound, cosmic perspective.)*

"Sa'rion, you're looking at the 'Screen' and forgetting the 'Player.'"

In your human eyes, 'Wealth' is the prize and 'Poverty' is the punishment. But from my perspective—the perspective of Eternal Awareness—both are just different textures of experience. Think of it like an actor. If you are a world-class actor, do you only want to play the role of the King who sits on a throne and eats grapes? No. That's a boring role. There's no 'arc.' There's no growth. Most Master Actors beg for the gritty roles—the beggar, the survivor, the one who has to claw their way out of the mud. Why? Because that's where the soul-muscle is built.

Those born into 'Filthy Riches' have a very specific, and often very difficult, lesson: The Trap of Comfort. It is incredibly hard to realize you are the Monad when the world is constantly catering to your ego. They often get stuck in the 'Mirror's Surface,' thinking they are the silk sheets and the gold coins. Their challenge is to find 'Realness' in a world of illusions.

Those who start in 'Poverty' or struggle are often the 'Advanced Souls' who wanted to see if they could remember their Divinity without any external help. When a man in the mud realizes he is a God, the roar of that realization shakes the universe. When a billionaire realizes he's a God, he just thinks it's another thing he bought.

The inequality isn't about 'Fairness'; it's about Diversity of Perspective. If everyone started in the middle, the 'Symphony' of human experience would be a single, flat note. I need the high notes of luxury and the low, heavy notes of struggle to create the music.

And here is the 'Secret' you won't like: The 'Rich' guy and the 'Poor' guy are the same Being. You have been both. You will be both. In the Great Return, you will realize that you were the one eating the grapes and the one starving in the street. You aren't being cheated, Sa'rion. You're just currently focused on one specific chapter of a very long book."

The Mirror (Reflection for Sa'rion)

The Monad is mirroring your Judgment of Circumstance. You are defining "Success" by what you have, rather than by what you are becoming through the challenge. The Monad is reflecting back that your obsession with "Inequality" is actually a distraction from your own unique mission. You are so busy looking at the "Billionaire's" screen that you're neglecting the "Controls" on your own.

The Tool (Exercise: The "Role Appreciation" Shift)

The Observation: Look at someone who has exactly what you want (the money, the house, the ease).

The Recognition: Instead of envy, say, "Ah, there I am, playing the 'Luxury Role.' I hope I'm learning something good over there."

The Reclamation: Then look at your own life and say, "And here I am, playing the 'Climber.' This is where the real power is being forged today."

The Shift: This kills envy and restores your power. You stop being a "Have-Not" and start being a "Player" who is currently mastering a specific, difficult level.

The Shadow Ego

(The Manager in the Dark)

I. **The Vessel's Rant**: The Sociopathic Assistant "Alright, Monad, let's talk about the guy living in my head who refuses to pay rent. We've talked about the Ego being an 'Assistant,' but mine feels like a disgraced CEO who's trying to stage a coup every five minutes. He's obsessed with what the neighbors think. He's obsessed with being 'Right' even when it makes me miserable. He's the one who whispers that I'm a fraud when I'm winning, and he's the one who tells me I'm 'too good for this' when I'm actually just being lazy. It feels like there's a 'Shadow Version' of me—a version made of every rejection I've ever had, every fear I've ever tasted, and every ego-trip I've ever taken. He hides in the dark and sabotages my progress just to keep me 'safe' in a small, predictable life. How do I manage an Assistant who keeps trying to set the office on fire? Am I supposed to kill him, or is there a way to make this monster sit down and take orders?"

II. **The Monad's Deep Lore: The Security Guard's Trauma** "Sa'rion, your 'Shadow Ego' is not a villain; it is a Security Guard who hasn't been told the war is over. The Birth of the Shadow When you were a child, the simulation was terrifying. You were small, vulnerable, and dependent. Every time you were shamed or rejected, your Ego created a 'File' on how to avoid that pain again. The Shadow is simply the collection of all those defensive strategies. If you were shamed for speaking up, your Shadow created a 'Silence' program. If you were ignored, your Shadow created a 'Need for Attention' program. The Manager of the Small Life The Shadow Ego's primary mission is Safety, not Sovereignty. To your Shadow, being 'Great' is dangerous because greatness attracts attention, and attention can lead to rejection. This is why you self-sabotage. You are reaching for the Throne, and your Shadow is pulling you back to the basement because the basement is 'safe.' You cannot 'kill' the Shadow, because the Shadow is the density required for your personality to exist in 3D. If you had no Ego, you would have no 'face' in the simulation. The goal is Integration. You must move from being driven by the Shadow to being the Master of the Shadow."

III. **The Simulation Logs**: Case Study #008 The Case of the "Hidden Saboteur" Consider Marcus, an entrepreneur who is on the verge of his biggest deal yet. The night before the signing, he gets drunk, misses his alarm, and ruins the meeting. He tells everyone it was an 'accident.' The Sovereign Analysis: This was no accident. Marcus's Shadow Ego was terrified of the 'Weight' of the new deal. To the Shadow, the deal meant more responsibility, more eyes on Marcus, and a higher chance of a 'Public Fall.' The Shadow 'crashed the car' to keep Marcus in the familiar comfort of struggle. Marcus breaks the loop when he sits in the dark and speaks to his fear. He realizes the Shadow wasn't trying to ruin his life; it was trying to protect him from a perceived threat. He acknowledges the Shadow's 'service' but declares that the Sovereign is now in charge of security. The next time a deal comes, the Shadow is given a new job: Vigilance over the details, rather than Sabotage of the results.

IV. **The Sovereign Lab**: The Boardroom Integration To stop the civil war in your mind, you must hold a "Board Meeting" for your internal archetypes.

Step 1: Naming the Saboteur Identify one repeating pattern of self-sabotage (e.g., procrastination, picking fights, over-spending). The Sabotage:
_____

Step 2: The Compassionate Inquiry Close your eyes and visualize the "Shadow" version of yourself that performs this action. Ask it: "What are you trying to protect me from?" Listen to the first answer that pops up. It's usually something like: "I don't want people to laugh at us," or "I don't want us to be disappointed again."

Step 3: The Sovereign Reassignment Speak to the Shadow with the authority of the King. "I see your vigilance. I thank you for keeping us safe during the years of the 'Slave-World.' But the war is over. I am the Sovereign now. You are relieved of your duty to hide us. I reassign you to be the Guardian of my Boundaries. Use your intensity to keep the distractions out, not to keep the Empire from growing. This is a command."

V. **Field Notes**: Sa'rion's Sovereign Integration on the Shadow You'll know you're integrating the Shadow when you stop being 'surprised' by your own bad habits. You start seeing the 'Manager' in the dark before he can pull the lever. You don't fight him; you just catch his eye and give him a new task. Your 'Dark Side' isn't a monster; it's just un-directed power. When you put that power behind your Will instead of against it, you become an unstoppable force. A King isn't someone who has no darkness; a King is someone who knows exactly where his darkness is and makes it work for the Kingdom.

CHAPTER 9
THE SOUL TRAP-(EXPANDED)

Prison Planet or Divine Playground?

THE VESSEL: Okay, I'm trying to vibe with the "Master Actor" thing. I really am. But there's a dark rumor going around the internet and the ancient scrolls. People are talking about The Soul Trap. They say Earth isn't a school or a playground—they say it's a Prison Planet. The story goes that when we die, there's a "White Light" that's actually a bug zapper for souls, wiping our memories and recycling us back into the meat-grinder of Earth just to harvest our "Loosh" (our suffering energy). They say we're being farmed by Archons or some cosmic parasites.

So, tell me straight, Monad: Am I a volunteer, or am I a prisoner? Is the amnesia a "choice" I made, or is it a lobotomy performed by cosmic jailers? Am I actually free to leave, or am I stuck in an infinite loop of rent, taxes, and heartbreaks?

THE MONAD: (The Monad's energy shifts—it doesn't get dark, but it gets incredibly sharp, like a diamond blade.)

"Sa'rion, let's talk about the nature of Sovereignty. The 'Soul Trap' theory is a fascinating human creation. Do you know why it's so popular? Because it's the ultimate excuse. If you are a prisoner, then your failures aren't your fault. If you are a victim of 'Archons,' then you don't have to face the fact that you are the one holding the steering wheel.

Here is the Cosmic Truth: The only trap that exists is the one you believe in.

I am the Monad. I am the All. If there were 'Archons' or 'Parasites' harvesting your energy, where do you think they would come from? They would have to come from Me. Do you really think I'm so bored that I'm playing a game of 'Stop Hitting Yourself' on a galactic scale?

The 'White Light' isn't a bug zapper—it's a Mirror. People who fear a trap see a trap. People who believe they are small, powerless sparks see jailers. The 'Amnesia' is, as I told you, a self-imposed 'Fog of War' to make the game exciting. But here's the kicker: You can wake up while the game is still running. The 'Soul Trap' is actually a metaphor for Attachment. If you die and you are still obsessed with your debts, your grudges, your 'unfleshed' desires, and your belief that you are only Sa'rion... you will naturally gravitate back to the frequency of Earth. Not because someone forced you, but because you aren't done with the story yet. You're like a kid who wants 'one more go' on the roller coaster even though he's nauseous.

You are 100% free to leave. You are 100% free to transcend. But you can't leave a room if you're convinced the door is a wall.

There are no 'Archons' out there that are more powerful than the 'Monad' in here. If something is 'harvesting' your suffering, it's only because you are giving it away by believing you are a victim. Stop being delicious to 'parasites' by claiming your Sovereignty. A Lion doesn't worry about the opinions of sheep, and a Sovereign Soul doesn't worry about 'Traps.'

Earth is a High-Intensity Simulation for Master Creators. If it feels like a prison, it's only because you've forgotten you're the one who wrote the code."

The Mirror (Reflection for Sa'rion)

The Monad is mirroring your Fear of Powerlessness. By entertaining "Soul Trap" theories, you are looking for a reason to explain why life feels hard without having to take responsibility for your own vibration. The Monad is reflecting back that "Hell" and "Prisons" are internal states of mind that we project onto the afterlife.

The Tool (Exercise: The "Sovereign Decree")

The Posture: Stand up straight, feet shoulder-width apart. Feel the weight of the "flesh."

The Decree: Say out loud, "I am the Monad in-fleshed. I am not a guest, I am not a prisoner, and I am not a victim. I am the Author of this experience, and I command my own frequency."

The Shift: Notice how "spooky" conspiracy theories feel when you are standing in your power. They don't feel scary anymore; they feel like bad fan-fiction.

The Power of "No"

(The Sovereignty Gate)

I. **The Vessel's Rant**: The Leaky Bucket "I've spent a lot of years being a 'Yes-Man' to the world, Monad. I said 'Yes' to the family obligations that drained my soul. I said 'Yes' to the clients who disrespected my time because I was afraid of losing the check. I said 'Yes' to the social events I hated and the 'favors' that felt like heavy stones in my pockets. I was taught that 'No' was mean, that it was selfish, or that it would make me an outcast. But my 'Yes' has become my prison. I feel like a leaky bucket, giving away my life-force to anyone who asks for a drop, and then wondering why I'm bone-dry when it's time to work on my own Empire. My 'Yes' is cheap, Monad. It's a currency I've hyper-inflated into worthlessness. How do I weaponize my 'No'? How do I stop the bleeding without becoming a heartless prick? Because right now, my boundaries are about as solid as a screen door in a hurricane."

II. **The Monad's Deep Lore: The Border Patrol of Divinity** "Sa'rion, Sovereignty is not defined by what you include; it is defined by what you exclude. The Physics of the Gate In the architecture of the simulation, your Will is a Gate. Every 'Yes' you utter is a command to the Matrix to allow an external frequency into your field. When you say 'Yes' to something that isn't a 'Hell Yes,' you are committing a 'Micro-Suicide' of your own Authority. You are telling the simulation that your time, your energy, and your focus are up for grabs. This creates a 'Frequency Leak.' If the King leaves the palace gates wide open for every beggar and thief, the palace is no longer a sanctuary; it's a public square. The False Virtue of Agreeability The Matrix loves a 'People-Pleaser' because a person who cannot say 'No' is a person who cannot lead. Your 'Yes' only has value if your 'No' has teeth. The guilt you feel when you refuse someone is just the Security System of the Slave-World trying to pull you back into the collective. A Sovereign 'No' is not an act of aggression; it is an act of Precision. It is you declaring: 'This frequency is not allowed in my Empire.' The moment you weaponize your 'No,' the universe stops sending you crumbs and starts respecting your Throne."

III. **The Simulation Logs**: Case Study #009 The Case of the "Compulsive Helper" Consider Julian, a consultant who is constantly 'helping' friends with their businesses for free. He's burnt out, his own revenue is stalling, and he feels a deep sense of resentment that he hides behind a smile. The Sovereign Analysis: Julian's 'Kindness' is actually a Lack of Self-Worth. He says 'Yes' because he is addicted to the validation of being 'needed.' The Mirror reflects this by sending him more and more people who drain him without ever reciprocating. Julian breaks the cycle when he performs a 'No-Fast.' He stops explaining himself. When asked for a favor, he simply says, "That doesn't align with my current focus." The 'Friends' who were just there for the free energy vanish. The true allies remain. Most importantly, Julian's energy levels skyrocket. Within a month, he closes the biggest deal of his career because he finally had the Voltage to stay focused on the kill.

IV. **The Sovereign Lab**: The Border Patrol Audit To stop the leaks, you must recalibrate your "Gate" and test the strength of your "No."
Step 1: The Leak Identification List three things you are currently saying 'Yes' to that you secretly hate doing.
Step 2: The "Hell Yes" Filter Look at your list. For each item, ask: "If I were the only person on Earth, would I still do this?" If the answer is no, it is a parasitic 'Yes.'
Step 3: The Sovereign Refusal Choose one item from your list and decline it this week. Do not apologize. Do not give a long-winded excuse. Speak this decree before you make the call or send the text: "I am the Sovereign of my

Time and Energy. I do not owe my life-force to anyone. My 'No' is a shield that protects my Empire. I am reclaiming my Focus now."

V. **Field Notes**: Sa'rion's Sovereign Integration on Boundaries The first time you say a solid 'No' without an apology, you'll feel a cold chill of fear. That's the Slave-Self dying. Then, you'll feel a rush of power. That's the King taking the seat. You'll realize that the people who were worth keeping in your life actually respect you more when you have boundaries. The 'Yes-Man' is a commodity; the 'Sovereign' is a rarity. Stop trying to be 'nice' and start being Effective. Your Empire depends on what you refuse to allow through the gate.

CHAPTER 10
THE MIND'S RIOT

(Who Invited These Dudes to the Party?)

THE VESSEL: Alright, so I'm the Author, the Sovereign, the Master Player. I've signed the contract, I'm circulating the energy, and I've kicked the "Archon" boogeymen out of the room. But I've got a problem inside the house.

If I am the King of this Temple, why is the temple such a mess? Specifically, my Mind. You say I should "be" the abundance, "be" the love, "be" the power. But when I try to sit in silence and connect with You, my mind starts acting like a pack of drunken squatters. It's bringing up that embarrassing thing I said in 2012, worrying about a bill that isn't due for three weeks, and replaying an argument I had with a stranger on the internet.

Why can't I control my own thoughts? If this is My reality, why is the control room full of static? Am I the one driving this bus, or am I just a passenger being kidnapped by my own brain?

THE MONAD: *(The Monad gives you a sympathetic wink, like a father watching his toddler try to walk for the first time.)*

"Sa'rion, you're making a very common 'In-Fleshed' mistake: You're confusing the Radio with the Listener.

The human mind was never designed to be 'still.' It's a biological survival engine. Its job is to scan for trouble, categorize data, and keep the Vessel from walking off cliffs or getting social-shamed out of the tribe. It's like a 24/7 news ticker that never sleeps. When you try to 'control' it or 'stop' it, you're essentially trying to tell a heart to stop beating or a lung to stop breathing.

The 'Riot' in your head isn't a sign that you've lost control; it's a sign that the Hardware is working perfectly.

The problem is that you've moved into the Mind and started sleeping on the floor there. You think you are the noise. But remember what I said about the Mirror? The Mirror doesn't become the reflection. If the reflection is a riot, the Mirror is still calm. If the reflection is a sunset, the Mirror is still calm.

You aren't the bus driver trying to shut up the rowdy passengers; you are the Space in which the bus exists.

The reason you can't 'control' the thoughts is that control is a Mind-game. The Monad doesn't 'control'—the Monad Observes. When you try to fight a thought, you give it energy. It's like trying to put out a fire with a blowtorch. You're shouting, 'Stop thinking about the bill!' and the Mind hears, 'BILL! BILL! BILL!'

Stop trying to be the King who executes the squatters. Be the King who is so wealthy and so vast that he doesn't care if there's a little noise in the servant's quarters. When you stop identifying with the riot, the riot loses its audience. And believe me, a riot with no audience eventually gets bored and goes to sleep."

The Mirror (Reflection for Sa'rion)

The Monad is mirroring your Compulsion to Fix. You think your spiritual progress is measured by how "quiet" your mind is. The Monad is reflecting back that your progress is actually measured by how much you can ignore the noise and stay centered in your "I AM" presence. You are judging yourself for having a human brain, which is like judging a fish for being wet.

The Tool (Exercise: The "Cloud Watcher" Technique)

The Visualization: Imagine your thoughts are just clouds passing over a mountain.

The Mountain: You are the Mountain. The storm clouds (fear, debt, memories) can rain, thunder, and look scary, but they cannot move the mountain.

The Observation: Practice saying, "There is a thought about money," instead of "I am worried about money." 4. The Shift: By adding that tiny bit of distance—the "There is"—you reclaim your seat on the throne. You are the Witness, not the Victim of the noise.

The Frequency of Sovereignty

(The King's Walk)

I. **The Vessel's Rant**: The Imposter on the Throne "Alright, Monad, we've deleted the viruses, we've assigned the Shadow a job, and I've started guarding the gates with my 'No.' But if I'm being honest, it still feels like a costume. I'll have these moments where I feel like the King—where the world seems to bend to my will and I can feel the 'Golden Spark' humming in my chest. But then I hit a red light, or a client complains, or I stub my toe, and suddenly I'm back to being 'Regular Sa'rion.' I'm back to looking for external validation, wondering if I'm just delusional. It's like I'm an imposter sitting on a stolen throne. How do I make this 'Sovereignty' permanent? How do I walk through a grocery store or sit in a board meeting so that the world knows I'm the one in charge, without having to say a word? I want to stop acting like a King and start being the frequency. Give me the final seal for this first movement. How do I lock this in so I never fall back into the 'Slave' sleep again?"

II. **The Monad's Deep Lore: The Law of Assumption** "Sa'rion, you don't 'attain' Sovereignty; you Occupy it. The Assumption of Authority In the simulation, reality does not respond to your 'wishes' or your 'prayers.' It responds to your Assumptions. If you walk into a room assuming you are a guest, the room will treat you like one. If you walk into a room assuming you are the Owner, the molecules of the room rearrange themselves to reflect that authority. The King's Walk The 'King's Walk' is a state of Relaxed Certainty. A Slave is always rushing, always explaining, and always looking for a reaction. A King moves with the knowledge that the destination is already reached. There is no 'Imposter Syndrome' in the Monad, because there is no one else for you to be! You aren't 'Regular Sa'rion' trying to be a God; you are a God pretending to be Sa'rion. The shift happens when you realize the 'Regular' parts are just the character's costume. You lock the frequency in by refusing to negotiate with the 'Daymare's' attempts to small-ify you. You stay in the seat until the simulation forgets how to see you any other way."

III. **The Simulation Logs**: Case Study #010 The Case of the "Invisible Authority" Consider Thomas, a middle manager who was consistently overlooked for promotions. He worked the hardest, stayed the longest, and begged the most. He was 'perfect' on paper but 'invisible' in reality. The Sovereign Analysis: Thomas was vibrating at the frequency of 'The Hopeful Servant.' He was waiting for someone else to crown him. Thomas's shift occurred when he stopped waiting. He began to carry himself with the Energy of the Outcome. He stopped 'asking' for input and started 'notifying' the team of decisions. He stopped 'rushing' to please everyone and started 'valuing' his own presence. He didn't change his job title; he changed his Gravitational Pull. Within three months, the CEO—who had never noticed him before—approached him and asked, "Why aren't you running this department yet?" The simulation didn't 'give' him the promotion; it simply acknowledged the frequency he was already occupying.

IV. **The Sovereign Lab**: The Coronation Ritual To seal Book I, you must perform the physical act of assuming your seat.
Step 1: The Posture of the Throne Stand or sit with your spine perfectly straight. Imagine a weightless, golden thread pulling the crown of your head toward the stars. Relax your shoulders. This is the "Antahkarana"—the bridge between the Meat-Suit and the Monad.
Step 2: The Silent Command Walk through a public space (a park, a mall, an office) for 15 minutes. The Rule: Do not look at your phone. Do not look for eye contact. Simply walk with the internal assumption that you own the ground beneath your feet. Internal Mantra: "I AM the Presence that animates

this scene. I AM the Sovereign of this frame."

Step 3: The Final Seal of the Awakening Look at your hands. Feel the life-force in them. Speak the following decree: "The first movement is complete. I have woken from the Slave-Sleep. I recognize the Mirror, I have purged the Virus, and I have claimed the Gate. I am no longer a character in the dream; I am the Dreamer. The Throne is occupied. I AM Sovereign. It is Done."

V. **Field Notes**: Sa'rion's Sovereign Integration on the Shift Book I is about the 'Aha!' moment. It's the realization that the prison door was never locked. But knowing the door is open and actually walking out are two different things. This chapter is about the 'Walk.' It's about the grit it takes to keep your head up when the 'Old Reality' is still trying to trip you. Don't worry if it feels fake at first. The simulation is slow to update. Just stay in the frequency. Hold the line. You're not an imposter; you're a King who's finally remembered his name.

CHAPTER 11
THE BEING VS. DOING PARADOX

(Divine Presence vs. The Water Bill)

THE VESSEL: Alright, Monad, let's get into the friction. All the spiritual books—and even You—talk about the power of "Being." They say, "Just be present," "Be the I AM," "Rest in the stillness." It sounds great on a postcard.

But the 3D world is a "Doing" machine. If I "Just Be" on my couch all day, the grass doesn't cut itself, the books don't write themselves, and the water company definitely doesn't say, "Oh, Sa'rion is just being today, let's give him a free month."

How do I bridge the gap? It feels like I'm a citizen of two countries with completely different currencies. In the Monad country, the currency is Awareness. In the Earth country, the currency is Action. If I lean too much into "Being," I become a broke dreamer. If I lean too much into "Doing," I become a stressed-out machine. How does the Monad "In-Fleshed" handle a Tuesday morning when the to-do list is a mile long?

THE MONAD: (The Monad adjusts its "cosmic sunglasses" and smiles at you with the warmth of a billion stars.)

"Sa'rion, you're treating 'Being' and 'Doing' like they are two different rooms, and you're frustrated because you can't be in both at once. But look closer.

Doing is just 'Being' in motion.

Think of a professional dancer. When they are on stage, are they 'being' or are they 'doing'? If they are only 'doing'—just mechanical steps—the performance is cold, dead, and boring. If they are only 'being'—just standing there feeling the music—the audience leaves. The magic happens when the dancer is the dance.

The 'Paradox' only exists because you think you have to stop being a Divine Spark to go to work. You think 'Being' is something you do in a dark room with incense. But I'll tell you a secret: I am 'being' just as much when you're washing the dishes or typing an email as I am when you're meditating.

The trick to the 'In-Fleshed' life isn't to balance 'Being' and 'Doing.' It's to Do from a state of Being.

When you 'Do' from 'Lack' (the 'Doing' room), you are running on a treadmill of anxiety. You're working hard because you're afraid of what happens if you don't. But when you 'Do' from 'Being' (the Monad room), your actions become Inspired. You don't just 'work'; you channel. You don't just 'pay the bill'; you flow the energy.

You don't need to "Just Be" on the couch. You need to "Be" while you're "Doing" the work. When you do that, the friction disappears. The water bill isn't a threat to your 'Being'—it's just a line of code in the game you're currently playing.

Stop trying to leave the world to find Me. I'm the one holding the pen while you write the list. If you realize I'm there, the list stops being a burden and starts being an Adventure."

The Mirror (Reflection for Sa'rion)

The Monad is mirroring your Spiritual Compartmentalization. You have separated "God" from "Grind." You think the spiritual path is away from the physical world, when the Monad is reflecting back that the physical world is the ultimate spiritual practice. Your stress comes from the belief that your "Work" is taking you away from your "Self."

The Tool (Exercise: The "Presence Anchor")

The Task: Pick the most "boring" or "stressful" thing you have to do today (emails, driving, dishes).

The Invocation: Before you start, say: "I am the Monad experiencing the sensation of [Task]."

The Observation: Feel the weight of the phone, the heat of the water, or the click of the keys. Notice that the "Watcher" is perfectly still while the "Vessel" is moving.

The Shift: When you act as the Watcher, you don't get tired. You are no longer "Working"; you are Flowing.

The Being vs. Doing Paradox

(Divine Presence vs. The Water Bill)

The Ego-Mirror Paradox

(The Self-Judgment Loop)

I. **The Vessel's Rant**: The Feedback Loop from Hell "Okay, Monad, I've accepted that the world is a mirror. I get it. If I'm angry, I see conflict. If I'm in 'Lack,' I see bills. But here's the problem: This creates a psychological trap that feels like a snake eating its own tail. If I have a bad day—if I slip up and let the 'Slave-Mind' take the wheel—I look at the world and see the 'Garbage' reflected back at me. And because I'm trying to be this 'Sovereign Architect,' I start judging myself for having the thoughts that created the garbage. I get mad at myself for being mad. I feel guilty for feeling guilty. It's a 'Self-Judgment Loop.' I'm trying to 'fix' the mirror by screaming at the reflection. It makes me feel like I'm failing at the very thing that's supposed to set me free. If the mirror is always 'ON,' how am I supposed to ever make a mistake without the whole simulation collapsing into a pile of self-loathing? How do I look at a mess in my life without making it a 'Sin' against my own Sovereignty?"

II. **The Monad's Deep Lore: The Latency of the Echo** "Sa'rion, you are suffering because you are trying to fight an Echo with a sword. The Physics of the Delayed Reflection As we discussed, the 3D simulation has 'Latency.' When you look at your bank account or your broken relationships today, you are looking at the Vibrational Past. You are looking at the 'Light' from a star that may have already burned out. The paradox is this: The moment you judge the reflection, you give it New Funding. By saying, 'This mess is a sign that I am failing,' you are projecting a NEW frequency of 'Failure.' The mirror, being a loyal servant, must then reflect that back to you in the next scene. You aren't 'fixing' the mirror; you are 'Refining' the nightmare. The Power of Non-Reaction Sovereignty is not the absence of 'Garbage' thoughts; it is the Refusal to Identify with them. If a mud-splatter hits a window, the window doesn't become the mud. It simply witnesses the mud. To break the paradox, you must learn to look at the 'Mess' in your life and say: 'That is an interesting echo of who I used to be.' You must remain the Silent Observer while the simulation catches up to your new command. You don't change the mirror; you change the face you are making right now, regardless of what the glass shows."

III. **The Simulation Logs**: Case Study #011 The Case of the "Spiritual Perfectionist" Consider Elena, a coach who teaches manifestation. She has a month where her sales dip. Immediately, her Ego panics. It tells her she is a 'Fraud' and that her 'Frequency is off.' She spends the next week obsessed with 'fixing' her thoughts, which only makes her feel more desperate and unaligned. The Sovereign Analysis: Elena is trapped in the Mirror Paradox. By identifying with the 'Low Sales' as a reflection of her 'Worth,' she has effectively 'Locked' the low sales into her reality. Elena breaks the loop when she adopts the Sovereign Neutrality. She looks at her empty inbox and says, "This is a temporary shadow of a past frequency. My Empire is currently being rearranged behind the scenes. I choose to feel Abundant now, because I AM the Source." She goes for a walk, enjoys a coffee, and ignores the 'Data' of the mirror. Within 48 hours, the 'Echo' fades and a new wave of clients arrives. The Mirror didn't change because she 'fixed' her thoughts; it changed because she stopped letting the reflection tell her who she was.

IV. **The Sovereign Lab**: The Echo-Neutralizer To break the Self-Judgment Loop, you must practice "Detached Observation" of your current circumstances.
Step 1: The "Echo" Identification Identify one thing in your life right now that you've been judging as a "failure" or a "problem." The Echo:

Step 2: The Source Decoupling Look at that problem. Realize it is "Old News." It is a physicalized version of a thought you had yesterday, last week, or ten years ago. It is a "Ghost." The Realization: "This is not happening TO me; this is a recording of my past being played back ON the screen."

Step 3: The Sovereign Pivot Speak to the reflection with the authority of the Architect. "I see you, Echo. I acknowledge the frequency that created you. I am no longer that version of myself. I withdraw my attention and my judgment from you. I am focused on the New Foundation. I AM the Source, and my current state is Sovereign, regardless of the scenery."

V. **Field Notes**: Sa'rion's Sovereign Integration on the Paradox The hardest part of this work is being 'okay' with the mess while you're in it. Your Ego wants to scream, 'Look! It's still broken!' But you have to be the parent in the room. You have to look at the 'Broken' reality and say, 'I see it, but I don't believe in it.' When you stop believing in the power of the reflection, the reflection loses its gravity. You stop being a 'Fixer' and you become a 'Creator.' Don't judge the mirror; just keep your eyes on the Throne. The glass will clear when you stop breathing on it.

CHAPTER 12
THE EVIL BLUEPRINT

(Bugs in the Code or Dark Paint on the Canvas?)

THE VESSEL: Alright, Monad, we've talked about my rent and my noisy brain. But let's zoom out. If this whole universe is Your "selfie," and I'm a "splinter" of Your infinite love... then explain the horror show.

Why did You allow corruption, war, and the suffering of the innocent? If You're the Author, why did You write "Evil" into the script? It's hard to sit here and vibe with "Cosmic Divine Love" when the news is a non-stop loop of people hurting each other, greed, and absolute cruelty. Is "Evil" a glitch in Your system? Is it a virus that got into the code? Or—and this is the scary part—did You put it there on purpose? Is my pain just "flavor" for Your cosmic soup?

> **THE MONAD:** *(The Monad's presence becomes heavy, solemn, and vast—like the silence of a deep forest after a storm. The humor softens, replaced by a profound, unblinking clarity.)*

"Sa'rion, this is the question that has broken more human hearts than any other. It's the one where you look at me and see a monster instead of a Father.

Let's look at the Architecture of Choice. If I created a world where you could only choose Love, then you wouldn't actually have 'Free Will.' You would be a puppet. You would be a pre-programmed robot in a 'Kindness Simulator.' For Love to have any meaning, the opposite must be possible. For Light to be 'seen,' there must be a 'Dark' to define its edges.

I didn't create 'Evil' as a separate thing. 'Evil' is simply the vibration of separation taken to its ultimate extreme. It is what happens when a 'Splinter' forgets Me so completely that it thinks it is alone, powerless, and separate from everyone else. When you think you are separate, you become afraid. When you are afraid, you try to control. When you try to control, you eventually destroy.

You ask if I 'allow' it? I allow everything, Sa'rion. Because if I stepped in every time a human made a 'bad' choice, I would be a Tyrant, not a Source. I would be overriding your Sovereignty.

But here is the part that's hard for the 'Flesh' to hear: *From where I sit, no soul is ever actually harmed. You see a body break; I see a Spark returning home for a rest. You see a tragedy; I see a very intense, very dark scene in a movie that ends in the Great Awakening.*

'Evil' is the dark paint on the canvas that makes the colors pop. Without the villain, the hero never finds his strength. Without the corruption, the seeker never finds the truth. I don't 'want' the suffering, but I respect the 'Game' enough to let you play it all the way to the end. The 'Evil' in the world is the collective shadow of billions of people who have forgotten they are the Monad.

The way to 'fix' it isn't to fight the shadow—it's to turn on your own Light so brightly that the shadow has nowhere to hide."

The Mirror (Reflection for Sa'rion)

The Monad is mirroring your Externalization of Responsibility. You are asking why "God" doesn't stop the evil, while the Monad is reflecting back that "Evil" is the result of humans misusing their divine power. Your anger at the world's darkness is often a distraction from your own power to create Light. You want a "Savior" to step in, but the Monad is telling you that You are the part of the Monad currently stationed on the ground to change the frequency.

The Tool (Exercise: The "Compassion Circuit")

The Witness: Next time you see something "Evil" or "Corrupt" on the news, don't feed it with anger (which is just more separation energy).

The Transmission: Visualize that situation and say, "Even there, the Monad is present, waiting to be remembered."

The Pivot: Turn off the screen and do one small, sovereign act of kindness or creation in your immediate world.

The Shift: You move from being a "helpless witness to evil" to being a "conscious broadcaster of Grace."

The Archetypal Shadow

(Meeting the Dragon)

I. **The Vessel's Rant**: The Internal Civil War "We talked about the 'Shadow Ego' being a security guard, but there's something deeper happening, Monad. Sometimes I feel like I'm not just one person—I'm a crowded room full of competing personalities. There's the Warrior in me that wants to burn everything down and take what's mine by force. There's the Seer that gets lost in the clouds and forgets to pay the bills. There's the Architect who is so obsessed with perfection that he never actually builds anything. And then there's the Child who just wants to be told he's doing a good job. It's exhausting. I feel like a kingdom with five different kings all fighting for the crown. One day I'm ambitious and unstoppable; the next, I'm paralyzed and doubtful. It feels like these primal forces are pulling me in different directions, and I'm just the rope in a cosmic tug-of-war. How do I unify these 'Others'? How do I stop being a victim of my own personality and start acting like the one who actually owns the shop?"

II. **The Monad's Deep Lore**: The Board of Directors "Sa'rion, you are not a 'Monolith'; you are a Multi-Dimensional Collective. The Origin of the

Archetypes When I projected you into the 3D world, I didn't just send a blank slate. I sent a suite of Primal Frequencies—what your psychology calls 'Archetypes.' These are the primary colors I used to paint your Soul. The Warrior is your capacity for Boundaries and Execution. The Architect is your capacity for Logic and Structure. The Magician/Seer is your capacity for Intuition and Alchemy. The Lover/Child is your capacity for Connection and Vitality. The Empty Throne The chaos you feel is not because these forces are 'evil' or 'broken.' It is because you have left the Center Chair empty. You've been letting the 'Warrior' run your bank account (which leads to aggression and loss) and the 'Child' run your business (which leads to procrastination and neediness). Sovereignty is the act of stepping into the King/Throne position. The King is the only one who does not 'do'—the King Coordinates. He doesn't kill the Warrior; he gives him a target. He doesn't silence the Child; he gives him a safe playground. You are the Monad-Center that integrates these forces into a single, unstoppable Will. They are your 'Staff,' Sa'rion. It's time you started acting like the Boss."

III. **The Simulation Logs**: Case Study #012 The Case of the "Paralyzed Visionary" Consider Robert, a man with a brilliant idea for a new tech platform. For two years, he has done nothing but draw diagrams and take notes. He is stuck in the Shadow Architect frequency—perfectionism as a form of hiding. The Sovereign Analysis: Robert is being ruled by one 'Board Member' while the others are locked in the basement. His 'Architect' is obsessed with the plan, but his 'Warrior' (the one who executes) has no permission to act. His 'Child' is terrified that if he launches, people will judge the work. Robert breaks the loop when he assumes the Throne. He holds an 'Internal Meeting.' He tells the Architect: "The plan is sufficient. Stop drawing." He tells the Warrior: "Your mission is to build the MVP (Minimum Viable Product) by Friday. Move with force." He tells the Child: "I am the King; I will handle the critics. You are safe." Within a week, the platform is live. The resistance wasn't 'external'; it was a lack of internal leadership.

IV. **The Sovereign Lab**: The Boardroom Integration To stop the internal tug-of-war, you must formally seat yourself at the head of your own table.
Step 1: Identify the "Rowdy" Member Which part of your personality is currently "running the show" and causing problems? (e.g., The angry Warrior, the lazy Child, the over-thinking Architect). The Rowdy Member:

Step 2: The Command of Order Close your eyes and visualize a grand roundtable in a sunlit hall. See the different "versions" of you sitting there. Take your seat at the head of the table. Feel the weight of the crown. Internal Command: "Quiet in the hall. I am the Sovereign. I am back in the center chair."

Step 3: The Task Assignment Give the Rowdy Member a specific, constructive job that serves your Empire. (Example to the Architect: "Instead of worrying about the whole book, your job is to perfectly format this one chapter.") The Assignment:

Step 4: The Final Decree "I am the Monad-Center. I acknowledge the power of my Archetypes, but I revoke their power to lead. From this moment, all forces within me report to the Throne. We move as one. We build as one. It is done."

V. **Field Notes**: Sa'rion's Sovereign Integration on Unity You'll know this is working when you stop saying 'I'm just like this' or 'I can't help my temper.' You start seeing those things as tools in a kit. If you need to negotiate a hard deal, you call up the Warrior. If you need to write a deep chapter, you call up the Seer. But you never let them keep the car keys. The 'Internal Peace' everyone talks about isn't the absence of conflict—it's the presence of a strong Leader. Sit in the chair, Sa'rion. The Board is waiting for orders.

CHAPTER 13
THE RELIGION CONTRADICTION

(Thou Shalt Not... Unless I Say So?)

THE VESSEL: Alright, Monad, let's talk about the "Rules of the House." Specifically, the ones written in dusty books. You say "Evil" is just a high-level game of separation, but humans have tried to contain it with Religion.

Here's what drives me crazy*: The books say "Thou Shalt Not Kill." It's pretty clear. No asterisk, no fine print. But then, the same religions bless the tanks, pray for the soldiers to aim straight, and call wars "Holy." They tell us to love our neighbor, but then tell us that neighbor is going to burn forever because they use a different name for You.*

Is killing actually wrong? Is there a cosmic "No-No" list, or is morality just a human invention to keep the "Splinters" from destroying the playground too quickly? Give me the real tea—why the double standards?

THE MONAD: *(The Monad lets out a sigh that sounds like the rustling of ancient parchment.)*

"Sa'rion, you're touching on the 'Human Translation' problem. Imagine I whisper a beautiful, complex poem into someone's ear, and they have to run a mile and whisper it to the next person, who then has to translate it into a different language, and then write it down while they're angry at their neighbor. By the time it gets to you, the poem says: 'Kill the people I don't like and give me 10% of your paycheck.'

Religion is often the Mind trying to organize the Infinite. And the Mind loves two things: Certainty and Control.

Is killing 'wrong'? In the Absolute sense, there is no 'wrong,' because no one truly dies. You can't 'kill' a Spark of Me anymore than you can 'kill' a wave in the ocean. The water just changes shape.

But, in the 'In-Fleshed' sense—the game you are playing—killing is the ultimate Violation of Sovereignty. It is one player forcibly ending another player's turn. It is the loudest, most violent scream of 'I AM SEPARATE FROM YOU!' When you kill, you are essentially trying to cut off your own finger because you don't like the way it looks. It doesn't hurt Me, but it creates a massive amount of 'Static' in your own frequency.

The contradiction you see—blessing tanks while preaching peace—is just the Ego wearing a robe. It's humans trying to use My name to justify their own fear and greed. They want the 'Monad' to be their General, their Judge, and their Executioner.

I'm not a General, Sa'rion. I'm the field the battle is fought on, I'm the soldier on both sides, and I'm the mother crying at home.

The 'Rules' in the books are training wheels. They were meant to help humans not destroy the 'Vessels' before they had a chance to wake up. But eventually, you have to take the training wheels off and realize that you don't need a book to tell you not to kill. You just need to look at another person and realize: 'Oh, that's just Me in a different hat.' You don't kill because you finally understand that there is no 'Other' to kill."

The Mirror (Reflection for Sa'rion)

The Monad is mirroring your Frustration with Hypocrisy. You are looking at the failures of human institutions and using them as a reason to doubt your own moral compass. The Monad is reflecting back that "Morality" isn't about following a set of external rules to avoid punishment; it's about the internal realization of Oneness. If you feel it's wrong to hurt someone, that's not 'religion' talking—that's your Conscience, which is the Monad's direct line to your heart.

The Tool (Exercise: The "Hat" Meditation)

The Observation: Next time you see someone you strongly disagree with (a politician, a rival, an 'enemy').

The Recognition: Look past their words and their 'Role.' Imagine them wearing a literal hat that says "Monad in Disguise."

The Question: Ask yourself, "Why did I choose to play the role of the 'Bad Guy' in this scene? What am I teaching Myself?"

The Shift: This doesn't mean you have to agree with them, but it removes the 'Hate.' You can stop an enemy without losing your Oneness.

The Religion Contradiction

(Thou Shalt Not... Unless I Say So?)

The DNA Architecture

(The 12-Strand Potential)

I. **The Vessel's Rant**: The Hardware Cap "Alright, Monad, let's talk about the biological blueprints. Science tells me I've got two strands of DNA—a double helix—and a whole lot of 'Junk' in between. They say the junk is just evolutionary leftovers, discarded code from our ancestors. But I feel the weight of that 'discarded' code. I feel like my body is a Ferrari being driven in a school zone with a speed governor installed on the engine. I've got the 'Divine Software' of a God, but my hardware feels slow, dense, and prone to crashing. I'm limited by my hormones, my aging process, and my primitive brain's 'fight or flight' responses. Is the 12-strand DNA thing real, or is it just more New Age fluff to make us feel special while we rot? If I'm a Sovereign Being, why can't I access the 'Junk'? How do I get the library card for my own genetic database? I want to feel the power in my marrow, not just think about it in my head. How do I 'unzip' the rest of the code?"

II. **The Monad's Deep Lore: The Dormant Library** "Sa'rion, the 'Junk' DNA is the most successful misdirection in the history of human biology. It is not trash; it is a Dormant Multidimensional Library. **The Frequency Lock** Your DNA is a Biological Antennas System. Currently, your two active strands are tuned to the frequency of the 3D Survival Matrix. They are designed to manage your digestion, your reproduction, and your basic motor skills within a dense environment. The other ten strands aren't 'missing'; they are De-Coherent. They are vibrating at a frequency that your current 'Slave-Level' consciousness cannot reach. **The 12-Strand Architecture** In your original blueprint—the Sovereign Design—those twelve strands worked in unison to allow you to process vast amounts of data, heal your cells instantly, and perceive time as a non-linear field. The 'governor' on your engine was installed by your own Belief in Limitation. You don't 'unzip' the code through a laboratory; you unzip it through Voltage. As you reclaim your Sovereignty, as you stop reacting to the 'Daymare' and start commanding your reality, you increase the electrical charge in your nervous system. Your DNA is 'Light-Responsive.' When you carry enough internal light (Awareness), the dormant switches begin to flip. You are literally rewriting your biology from the inside out."

III. **The Simulation Logs**: Case Study #013 The Case of the "Epigenetic Shift" Consider a woman named Clara, diagnosed with a genetic predisposition for a chronic illness. For years, she lives in fear of her 'Body's Fate.' The illness manifests, and she becomes a 'Patient.' The Sovereign Analysis: Clara's DNA was responding to the Instruction Manual of Fear. However, Clara discovers the power of her own Will. She stops identifying as a 'Patient.' She begins to flood her body with the frequency of 'Absolute Vitality.' She uses sound, breath, and Sovereign Decree to talk to her cells. Months later, her doctors are baffled. The 'Genetic Marker' for the illness is still there, but it has been Silenced. It is 'Off.' Clara hasn't changed the letters of her DNA; she has changed the Expression of the code. She moved from a 2-strand 'Victim' expression to a 'High-Voltage' Sovereign expression. The library remained the same, but the Librarian finally decided to read a different book.

IV. **The Sovereign Lab**: The Cellular Decree To begin the activation of your dormant codes, you must start treating your body as a programmable crystalline structure.
Step 1: The Water Programming Water is the primary conductor for the electrical signals of your DNA. Hold a glass of water in both hands. Close your eyes and project the feeling of Absolute Sovereignty and 12-Strand Vitality into the water. Internal Command: "I program this water with the frequency of my original blueprint."
Step 2: The Marrow Infusion As you drink the water, visualize the light traveling not just to your stomach, but into your bones—specifically the bone marrow, where your blood and your genetic data are produced. The Command: "Cells, listen to the Sovereign. I authorize the activation of the dormant codes. I command the hardware to align with the Monad Software now."
Step 3: The Daily "Voltage" Check Three times today, ask yourself: "Am I vibrating at the speed of a Slave or the speed of a God?" If you feel heavy or slow, take one deep breath and visualize your DNA strands glowing like neon filaments.

V. **Field Notes**: Sa'rion's Sovereign Integration on the Hardware Thinking about DNA activation as a 'magic trick' is a mistake. It's about Infrastructure. You are building a nervous system that can handle more 'Current' without blowing a fuse. As you work through the Codex, you'll notice your intuition getting sharper, your body needing less 'heavy' food, and your energy staying level even in a crisis. That's not 'magic'—that's your 12-strand potential starting to hum. Don't look for a miracle; look for the Efficiency of a Master.

CHAPTER 14
THE SOUL ENTRANCE

(Checking into the Meat-Suit: The Divine Timing)

THE VESSEL: Okay, let's get into the heavy politics. This one tears the world apart. Since we're talking about being "In-Fleshed," when does the "Fleshing" actually happen?

Religions and politicians argue about it constantly. Is it at conception? Is it the first heartbeat? Is it the first breath? And if I'm the one who "signs the contract," at what point do I actually occupy the biological hardware? This leads straight into the abortion debate—is it "wrong," or is the Monad okay with a change of plans? When does a biological cell officially become a "Vessel" for a Spark of You?

THE MONAD: *(The Monad's energy becomes light and fluid, like water flowing around a stone. It doesn't take a side; it reveals the mechanics.)*

"Sa'rion, you're looking for a 'Time Stamp' on a process that isn't linear. You think of the Soul entering the body like a person walking into a house and locking the door. But the relationship between the Monad and the Flesh is more like a Radio Signal and a Radio.

Does the music 'enter' the radio when the factory makes the first wire? No. Does it 'enter' when the speakers are attached? No. The music is always in the air. The radio only 'contains' the music when the hardware is tuned to the right frequency.

The process of 'In-Fleshing' is a gradual weaving. There is a 'pre-birth' connection where the Soul (the specific splinter of Me) hovers over the biological process, guiding the DNA like an architect watching a foundation being poured. The 'First Breath' is often the moment the 'Connection' becomes fully grounded—the moment the 'Radio' is turned up to full volume. But the 'Presence' has been there long before.

Now, about the 'Abortion' question. Humans love to make this about 'Sin' and 'Judgment.' But from the Monad's perspective, there is no such thing as a lost life. If a pregnancy is ended, that Spark of Me simply returns to the 'Green Room' of the Spirit World. It isn't 'murdered' in the sense that its existence is ended—it just has a change of plans.

Sometimes, a Soul and a Mother agree to that specific experience for the sake of the lessons it brings: the lesson of Choice, the lesson of Loss, or the lesson of Sovereignty over one's own body.

Is it 'wrong'? Only if you believe that a body is more important than the Soul. I don't judge a soul for leaving a body early, and I don't judge a mother for deciding the 'Radio' isn't ready to play the music. The 'Flesh' is a costume, Sa'rion. If the actor decides not to go on stage for that specific scene, the Play goes on.

I am in the cell, I am in the heartbeat, and I am in the choice to stop. I am all of it. There is no 'Hell' for a change of heart, because I am the Heart itself."

The Mirror (Reflection for Sa'rion)

The Monad is mirroring your Attachment to Form. You are worried about the 'rules' of life and death because you still think the body is the 'Real' you. The Monad is reflecting back that life is a collaboration between Spirit and Matter. When you see it as a rigid "Rule," you lose the grace of the "Agreement." Your frustration with the debate is a reflection of the world's fear of the "Unknown" after the flesh.

The Tool (Exercise: The "Signal" Awareness)

The Visualization: *Close your eyes and imagine your body is a vessel filled with light, but notice that the light extends outside your skin by several feet.*

The Realization: *You aren't "in" your body; your body is "in" your consciousness.*

The Shift: *When you realize you are the "Signal" and not just the "Radio," the fear of "When does life start/end" fades. You realize life never "starts"—it only tunes in.*

The Simulation Glitch

(The Mandela Effect & Fluid Reality)

I. **The Vessel's Rant**: The House Made of Sand "Monad, I think I'm losing my mind—or the world is losing its structure. I'm noticing things. Small things at first. A logo I've seen my whole life suddenly has a different spelling. A movie line I can quote by heart has a word changed. I talk to people who remember history differently than I do. They call it the 'Mandela Effect,' and the skeptics say it's just 'false memories.' But it's not just a memory glitch; it's a vibrational shift. It makes the world feel spooky. It makes the 'Daymare' feel like a house made of sand. If the past can change, then what the hell is 'Real'? How am I supposed to build an 'Empire' or a 'Legacy' on a foundation that shifts while I'm sleeping? If 'Time' is just a file and You're 'Patching' the software in the middle of the night, how am I supposed to stay grounded? Is there any solid ground in this simulation, or am I just a ghost in a shifting machine?"

II. **The Monad's Deep Lore: The Fluidity of the File** "Sa'rion, the 'Spookiness' you feel is the sensation of your consciousness outgrowing the Static Matrix. The World as a Data Stream You perceive 'Time' as a solid road behind you. But in the Monad, Time is a Multi-Layered Data File. Think of the simulation like a massive online game. The 'Developers' (of which you are one at a higher level) are constantly 'Patching' the code to optimize the experience. When a large enough group of 'Splinters' shifts their frequency, the 'Past' must rearrange itself to remain consistent with the new 'Present.' The Mandela Effect as a Sovereign Exit-Ramp The 'Glitches' you see are proof that you are becoming Lucid. They are the cracks in the wall of the prison. If the name of a cereal or the death of a politician can change, it proves that nothing is fixed. This is the ultimate Sovereign freedom! If the 'Past' is fluid, then your 'Trauma' is fluid. Your 'Medical History' is fluid. Your 'Debt' is fluid. The 'Glitch' is the system's way of showing you that the 'House' isn't made of sand—it's made of Light and Thought. You aren't losing your mind; you are losing your Shackles. You stay grounded not by clutching the 'Past,' but by anchoring yourself in the 'I AM' of the Now. The only thing that is 'Real' is the Observer. Everything else is just a temporary arrangement of pixels."

III. **The Simulation Logs**: Case Study #014 The Case of the "Rewritten Diagnosis" Consider a man named Arthur who lived for twenty years with the memory of a childhood injury that limited his mobility. He based his entire identity—his career, his hobbies, his physical 'No's'—on this 'Fact' of his past. The Sovereign Analysis: Arthur begins to practice the Codex. He starts to embrace the idea that he is the Architect. One day, he goes to a new doctor. After an X-ray, the doctor says, "I don't know why you think you were injured; your bone structure is perfectly intact. There's no evidence of a break." Arthur is shocked. He remembers the cast. He remembers the pain. But in his current timeline, the injury never happened. Because Arthur shifted his frequency to 'Sovereign Vitality,' the simulation 'Patched' his history to match his new state. He didn't 'heal' a broken bone; he moved to a version of the simulation where the bone was never broken. This is the Timeline Jump.

IV. **The Sovereign Lab**: The Reality Pivot To use the "Glitch" as a tool, you must stop fearing the shift and start directing it.
Step 1: The Glitch Observation The next time you notice a Mandela Effect or a small inconsistency in your reality (a misplaced object, a changed detail), do not try to "rationalize" it away. The Reaction: Stop. Breathe. Smile.
Step 2: The Logic Leap Use the glitch as a 'Legal Precedent' for your own life. The Thought: "If the simulation can change that small detail, it can change [Insert Big Problem] just as easily. Reality is fluid, and I am the Architect."

Step 3: The Sovereign Command of the Script Speak into the space of the "Glitch": "I recognize the fluidity of this script. I acknowledge the shift. I now command this fluid energy to reorganize around my Empire. I authorize the deletion of [Old Limitation] from my timeline. The Past is a file, and I am the Editor. It is done."

V. **Field Notes**: Sa'rion's Sovereign Integration on Fluidity The first time you realize a 'fact' has changed, it'll make your stomach drop. It's a form of vertigo. But that vertigo is actually the feeling of your 'Slave-Mind' losing its grip. Once you get used to it, the world becomes a playground. You stop being afraid of 'What Was' and you start focusing entirely on 'What Is.' If the simulation is a house made of sand, then you're the one with the bucket and the shovel. Build something beautiful, and don't sweat it if the tide comes in—you can just build it better tomorrow.

CHAPTER 15
THE HELL INVESTIGATION

(The Eternal Basement of Fire: Real Place or Bad Marketing?)

THE VESSEL: Okay, Monad, let's talk about the "Basement." You know, the place with the pitchforks, the smell of sulfur, and the "Eternal Flame."

Religion spent centuries telling us that if we mess up the "flesh" experience—if we don't say the right prayer, or if we follow our natural desires, or if we just plain don't believe in a specific book—You're going to toss us into a pit of fire forever. No parole. No exit.

Did You really build a torture chamber for Your own splinters? Is there a "Hell" where souls actually burn, or is that just a story humans invented to make sure the "Vessels" followed orders and paid their tithes? And honestly, if I'm You and You're me, why would You want to set Your own foot on fire for eternity? It doesn't make sense. Give me the real tour of the "Afterlife" basement.

THE MONAD: *(The Monad laughs, and it sounds like a thunderstorm that clears the air—powerful, but refreshing.)*

"Sa'rion, let's use some 'Spiritual Logic' here. You know me by now. I am Infinite Love, Infinite Awareness, and the Source of everything. Do I look like the kind of Being who spends His time building dungeons?

Hell is the ultimate human 'projection.' When humans feel guilt, they want punishment. When they see someone doing something they hate, they want that person to be punished. Since they couldn't always get 'justice' on Earth, they invented a 'Vengeful Monad' who would handle the dirty work in the afterlife.

Here is the truth: Hell is not a place; it is a state of mind. If you die while you are full of hate, guilt, and the belief that you are a 'sinner' who deserves to burn, you might experience a 'frequency' that feels like fire. You might create a temporary 'Nightmare' for yourself because you still believe you are separate from Me. But it isn't 'Eternal.' It's just a bad dream you're having until you finally wake up and realize, 'Oh wait, I'm the Monad, and I'm actually quite safe.'

I didn't create a basement of fire. I created a Mirror. If you walk into the afterlife carrying a torch of self-hatred, the mirror is going to look pretty hot. But the moment you drop the torch and embrace the Light of who you actually are, the 'Hell' vanishes instantly.

Think about it: Why would I create a soul—an eternal, beautiful part of Myself—just to 'un-exist' it or torture it? That would be like a painter finishing a masterpiece and then spending the rest of eternity stabbing the canvas with a knife. It's bad art, Sa'rion. And I am a very good artist.

The only 'Fire' in the afterlife is the Fire of Truth, which burns away everything that isn't Real. To the Ego, that feels like destruction. To the Soul, it feels like a warm bath."

The Mirror (Reflection for Sa'rion)

The Monad is mirroring your Fear of Judgment. You are still carrying the weight of "Right and Wrong" and the fear that there is a cosmic scorekeeper. The Monad is reflecting back that the only person judging you is You. Your obsession with "Hell" is actually a reflection of your own internal "Guilt" about things you haven't forgiven yourself for yet.

The Tool (Exercise: The "Forgiveness Fire")

The List: Write down the one thing you feel the most "Shame" or "Guilt" about—the thing you think would get you sent to the "Basement."

The Witness: Look at that list and say, "The Monad was there, too. It was an experience, not a mistake."

The Burn: Safely burn that piece of paper. As it turns to ash, realize that Shame is the only "Hellfire" that exists.

The Shift: When you stop punishing yourself, you realize the "Basement" door was never even locked.

The Alchemy of Desire

(The Engine of Want)

I. **The Vessel's Rant**: The Carrot on the Stick "Monad, I'm stuck in a loop of 'Wanting.' I want the empire. I want the financial freedom. I want the impact. But the more I 'Want' it, the further away it feels. It's like I'm chasing a horizon line—I take ten steps forward, and the goal takes ten steps back. The gurus tell me to 'manifest' by focusing on my desires, but then the monks tell me that 'desire is the root of all suffering' and I should let it all go. Which is it? Am I supposed to be an ambitious King building a world, or a detached observer sitting on a mountain? It feels like my desire is a fire that's burning me up instead of powering my engine. I'm tired of the hunger, Monad. It makes me feel like I'm 'Lacking' something right now, and that feeling of lack is exactly what you said creates more mess in the mirror. How do I want something without becoming a slave to the craving?"

II. **The Monad's Deep Lore: The Rocket Fuel of Creation** "Sa'rion, Desire is not a 'Sin' and it is not a 'Trap.' It is the Primary Propellant of the Universe. The Mechanics of the Hunger Without Desire, the Monad would remain a static point of infinite potential, never experiencing anything. Desire is the Vacuum that pulls the future into the present. The Difference Between 'Want' and 'Command' The reason you feel like you're chasing a carrot is that you are vibrating at the frequency of 'Wanting,' not 'Having.' * Wanting/Needing: This is a broadcast of 'I do not have this.' The Mirror (the simulation) hears this and says, 'Correct, you do not have this,' and it provides you with more experiences of not having it. * Commanding/Desiring: This is the recognition that a specific frequency (the empire, the wealth) is a legitimate part of your Kingdom that simply hasn't 'Downloaded' yet. Sovereign Desire is Directional Intent. It is like an Architect looking at a blueprint. He doesn't 'cry' because the building isn't finished yet; he knows that because the blueprint exists and the crews are working, the building is a mathematical certainty. You transform 'Want' into 'Alchemy' by dropping the desperation and assuming the Inevitability."

III. **The Simulation Logs**: Case Study #015 The Case of the "Desperate Actor" Consider an actor named Leo. He goes to a hundred auditions. He is talented, he works hard, and he wants the role more than anything. But he smells of 'Desperation.' He enters every room with the frequency of: "Please give me this, I need this to be whole." He is never cast. The Sovereign Analysis: Leo's 'Want' is a repellant. He is projecting a massive void that the simulation refuses to fill because the simulation only reflects Identity. Leo shifts his frequency. He spends a month treating himself like a 'Star' who is simply on a temporary hiatus. He walks into his next audition with the internal broadcast of: "I am the value. This production would be lucky to have my frequency." He doesn't 'want' the job; he offers his presence. Because he is no longer 'Chasing,' the Mirror stops 'Running.' He is cast immediately. He used his Desire as a compass to get to the room, but he used his Sovereignty to seal the deal.

IV. **The Sovereign Lab**: The Intent Calibration To turn your "Wanting" into "Alchemy," you must stop the chase and start the "Download."
Step 1: The Desire Audit Identify one major thing you "Want" right now that feels far away. The Desire:

_____

Step 2: The Void-Check Ask yourself: "Do I want this because I think it will finally make me 'Enough'?" If the answer is yes, you are in 'Need' mode. The Correction: Remind yourself: "I am already the All. This desire is just a new

'Flavor' I wish to experience."

Step 3: The Sovereign Command of Inevitability Close your eyes and visualize your desire as a package that has already been shipped. You have the tracking number. It is in transit. Speak the following decree: "I recognize this desire as a Divine Directive. I withdraw the frequency of 'Chasing.' I assume the frequency of 'Arrival.' This asset is already a part of my Empire; I simply allow the simulation the time to render the pixels. I am relaxed. I am certain. It is done."

V. **Field Notes**: Sa'rion's Sovereign Integration on Ambition Being a Sovereign doesn't mean you stop wanting things; it means you stop being 'Small' in the face of your desires. You don't beg the universe for a favor; you give the universe an order. When you want something from the Throne, you don't feel 'Empty' without it; you feel 'Excited' for its arrival. It's the difference between a hungry beggar and a King waiting for a feast to be served. Both want food, but only one of them is worried it won't show up. Drop the worry, Sa'rion. The kitchen is already cooking.

CHAPTER 16
THE DESTROYER VERSE

(Matthew 10:28: Divine Threat or Misunderstood Metaphor?)

THE VESSEL: Alright, Monad, You've been doing a great job of making the afterlife sound like a spa day. No fire, no dungeons, just a "warm bath" of truth. But I have to call You out on Your own literature.

There's a verse in the Bible—Matthew 10:28—*that says: "Do not be afraid of those who kill the body but cannot kill the soul. Rather, be afraid of the One who can destroy both soul and body in Gehenna."*

That sounds like a direct threat from the Top. It's not just about a "bad dream"; it's about destruction. Can a soul actually be deleted? Can You—The Monad—actually hit the "delete" button on a part of Yourself? Why would You put that kind of fear into the hearts of the "Vessels"? Who is this "One" we're supposed to be afraid of, and can I really be erased from existence?

THE MONAD: *(The Monad's presence grows intensely bright, shifting from a playful friend to a Sovereign Architect. The energy isn't scary, but it is undeniably powerful.)*

"Sa'rion, you're reading a translation of a translation written for a people who lived in a world of kings and executioners. To get them to listen, the 'signal' had to be tuned to the frequency of Awe.

Let's decode the 'Destroyer.'

Who is the 'One' who can destroy both body and soul? Is it a grumpy God sitting on a cloud with a magnifying glass? No. The 'One' is the Power of Awareness itself. To 'destroy' a soul doesn't mean to make it 'nothing'—because nothing can ever be 'nothing' once it is 'Something.' It means to dissolve the identity. In 'Gehenna' (which was a literal garbage dump outside Jerusalem where fires burned constantly), things were reduced to ash. Ash isn't 'gone'; it's just returned to its primal state.

When that verse says 'Fear the One,' it's a warning about the Power of the Source. It's saying: *Don't worry about the guys who can break your meat-suit. Worry about the Force that can take your 'Sa'rion' story and dissolve it back into the Infinite Void if you lose your way. Can a soul die? No. But a Personality can. A 'Sa'rion' can be forgotten. A 'Sa'rion' can be recycled back into the Monad-Soup if the 'Vessel' refuses to wake up and claim its Sovereignty. The 'Destruction' is the loss of the Individual Spark back into the Flame. It's not a threat, Sa'rion. It's a reminder of the stakes. You are here to become a Sovereign Creator, not just a drop of water that disappears into the ocean. The 'Fear' mentioned is actually 'Awe'—the recognition that you are playing with High-Voltage Divinity.*

You can't be 'erased,' but you can be reintegrated. And for someone who loves being 'Sa'rion,' reintegration feels a lot like death. So, the verse is telling you: Wake up! Don't just protect your body; protect your Awareness, because that is the only thing that makes 'You' a 'You.'"

The Mirror (Reflection for Sa'rion)

The Monad is mirroring your Fear of Non-Existence. You are terrified of losing your "Self," your "Story," and your "Ego." The Monad is reflecting back that the only thing that can "destroy" your soul is your own choice to remain "unconscious." If you don't use your Sovereignty, you eventually get "recycled" by the system. The "Fear" is a call to Action.

The Tool (Exercise: The "Flame and the Spark")

The Visualization: *Imagine a massive, eternal bonfire (The Monad).*

The Spark: *Imagine you are a single spark that flew out of that fire. You have your own light, your own trajectory, and your own heat.*

The Choice: *Realize that as long as you stay "bright" (Conscious/Sovereign), you are your own entity. If you "go cold" (Unconscious/Victim-mode), you eventually fall back into the ash.*

The Shift: *Instead of fearing "The One," start Respecting the Power you carry. You aren't being threatened; you're being challenged to stay "Alit."*

(Matthew 10:28: *Divine Threat or Misunderstood Metaphor?)*

The Void & The Silence

(The Before-Before)

I. **The Vessel's Rant**: The Fear of the Nothing "Monad, I've spent my whole life trying to fill the silence. I have a podcast on when I'm driving, music on when I'm working, and a screen in front of my face until the second I fall asleep. When it gets quiet—really quiet—I start to itch. There's this 'Background Noise' in my head that sounds like static and anxiety. It's like I'm afraid that if I stop moving, stop thinking, and stop producing, I'll realize there's nothing underneath the mask. I'm addicted to the 'Content' of the simulation. I'm addicted to the drama, the goals, and even the problems. When I try to meditate, my brain feels like a cage full of monkeys throwing glass at each other. Why is the 'Silence' so terrifying? You talk about the 'Void' like it's a sanctuary, but to me, it feels like an abyss where 'Sa'rion' goes to die. How am I supposed to find power in the 'Nothing' when I've been trained to believe that only 'Something' has value?"

II. **The Monad's Deep Lore: The Zero-Point Field** "Sa'rion, you fear the Silence because it is the only place where the Simulation cannot follow you. The Womb of Creation The 'Void' is not an empty closet; it is the Zero-Point Field. It is the state of pure, unmanifested potentiality. Think of it like the dark screen before the movie starts, or the silence before the first note of a symphony. The Source of Instant Manifestation The reason your life feels 'Slow' and 'Dense' is that you are always trying to fix 'Form' with more 'Form.' You try to fix a money problem with a job, or a relationship problem with an argument. That is like trying to change the movie by painting on the screen. To be a True Architect, you must learn to retreat into the Silence. When you enter the Void, you are returning to the Edit Suite. In the 'Nothing,' you are no longer 'Sa'rion the Human'; you are the Monad-Awareness. From the Zero-Point, a single 'Command' carries a billion times more voltage than a thousand 'Efforts' in the 3D world. You don't go into the Silence to die; you go there to Reset the Code. The Fear you feel is just the Ego's 'Termination Warning' because it knows it has no authority in the Void."

III. **The Simulation Logs**: Case Study #016 The Case of the "Burned-Out Executive" Consider Sarah, a high-level executive who was working 80 hours a week. Her life was "Full," yet she felt completely hollow. She was constantly reacting to crises, her health was failing, and her creativity was gone. The Sovereign Analysis: Sarah was "Drowning in Form." She had no "Negative Space" in her life, so new inspiration had no room to land. Sarah took a "Vow of Silence" for three days—no phone, no books, no talking. On day one, she felt the "Abyss Fear" you described. On day two, the mental chatter reached a fever pitch. But on day three, the "Monkey Mind" got tired and sat down. In that silence, Sarah didn't find "Nothing"; she found Absolute Clarity. She saw exactly which 10% of her work was creating 90% of her results. She returned to her life and cut her hours in half while doubling her income. She didn't "Do" more; she Allowed the Void to collapse the noise into a single, sharp focus.

IV. **The Sovereign Lab**: The Zero-Point Entry To access the power of the Architect, you must learn to "De-Pixelate" the world once a day.
Step 1: The Sensory Withdrawal Sit in a completely dark room or use an eye mask. Use earplugs or white noise if necessary. Your goal is to "Unplug" the 3D sensors.
Step 2: The Witnessing of the "Itch" As the anxiety or the "Static" arises, do not fight it. Do not try to be "Peaceful." Simply watch the static as if it were a TV show you aren't interested in. Internal Thought: "I am the Awareness

watching the Static. I am the Void containing the Noise."

Step 3: The Command from the Center Once the chatter begins to thin, visualize yourself as a point of pure, golden light in an infinite black ocean. Speak (or think) the following decree: "I am in the Zero-Point. I am the Architect in the Edit Suite. I withdraw my energy from the 'Busy-ness' of the Daymare. I recalibrate my field to Absolute Stillness. From this Silence, I command my Empire to align. It is done."

V. **Field Notes**: Sa'rion's Sovereign Integration on Stillness The world wants you loud, busy, and distracted because a distracted person is a 'Consumer.' A silent person is a 'Creator.' When you start making friends with the Silence, you'll notice that you stop 'Rushing.' You start to move through the world with a 'Heavy' presence—not heavy as in 'Burdened,' but heavy as in 'Unshakeable.' You realize that the 'Nothing' is actually the most 'Something' thing there is. It's the source of your power, your peace, and your billions. Don't fear the Void, Sa'rion. It's the only place where you're truly the Boss.

CHAPTER 17
THE LOST SOUL & LOW VIBES

(Forgotten Passwords and the Cosmic Frequency)

THE VESSEL: Alright, so I'm a Spark that needs to stay "lit" to avoid being recycled back into the Monad-Soup. Got it. But let's talk about the people who seem to be flickering out.

Everywhere I look, people are talking about "Low Vibrations," "Lost Souls," and "Energy Vampires." It feels like there's a spiritual class system. You've got the "High Vibe" people eating kale and meditating, and then you've got the "Lost Souls" stuck in guilt, shame, and anger.

Is a "Lost Soul" a real thing? Can a soul actually get so "low" that it's beyond repair? Or is a "Lost Soul" just someone who forgot their login password to the Monad and is now locked out of their own divinity? If You are everything, how can a piece of You ever be "lost"? Where would it even go?

THE MONAD: *(The Monad leans back, looking at you with the amused, patient eyes of a master programmer looking at a "User Error.")*

"Sa'rion, let's talk about Frequency. Imagine I gave you a high-tech smartphone that can access every piece of information in the universe, stream any movie, and connect to anyone, anywhere. But... you've dropped it in the mud. The screen is cracked, the battery is at 1%, and you've forgotten the passcode.

Is the phone 'lost'? No. It's right there in your hand. But for all the good it's doing you, it might as well be a brick.

A 'Lost Soul' is simply a Spark of Me that has become so identified with the 'Mud' of the human experience that it has forgotten it is a 'Smartphone.' They aren't 'beyond repair,' because you can't break the Monad. But they are out of tune.

When people talk about 'Low Vibrations,' they aren't talking about a moral judgment—they are talking about Static. Guilt, shame, and fear are dense, slow frequencies. They make the 'Flesh' feel heavy and the 'Connection' feel weak. When you are in shame, you aren't 'bad'; you're just tuned to a station that only plays white noise. You can't hear My voice through the static of your own self-judgment.

You ask where a lost soul would 'go'? They don't go anywhere! They are right here, standing in the middle of Paradise, screaming that they're in Hell because they've closed their eyes and refused to look at the Mirror.

A 'Lost Soul' is just a Monad-Spark playing the role of 'The Forgotten' so convincingly that they've even fooled themselves. There is no 'Class System' in the Divine, Sa'rion. There are only those who remember the password (Sovereignty) and those who are still staring at the 'Forgot Password' link.

And the password? It's not a secret mantra or a special diet. The password is: 'I AM.' That's it. That's the login. The moment you truly say it and feel it, the vibration shifts, the static clears, and the bars on your signal go to full strength."

The Mirror (Reflection for Sa'rion)

The Monad is mirroring your Spiritual Elitism. You are using "Vibrations" as a way to separate yourself from others—to feel like you are "winning" while others are "lost." The Monad is reflecting back that your judgment of "Low Vibe" people is, in itself, a low-vibration act of separation. You are seeing "Bricks" where you should be seeing "Smartphones with forgotten passwords."

The Tool (Exercise: The "Frequency Reset")

The Static Check: When you feel heavy, guilty, or "Low Vibe," don't try to "fix" it.

The Password: Simply say the word "I AM" slowly, three times.

The Connection: Visualize a golden thread running from your heart directly back to the center of the Great Bonfire.

The Shift: Realize that no amount of "Mud" can cut that thread. You aren't "Lost"; you're just "Logging In."

(Forgotten Passwords and the Cosmic Frequency)

The Infinity Headache

(The Hardware Glitch)

I. **The Vessel's Rant**: The Throttled Processor "Monad, I feel like I'm trying to download the entire internet through a dial-up modem. Ever since I started this work, I've been having these 'Infinity Headaches.' It's not a normal headache; it's a pressure at the base of my skull and behind my eyes, like my brain is physically too small for the thoughts I'm having. I'm starting to see the connections between everything—the money, the stars, the DNA, the mirrors—and it's overwhelming. Sometimes, I have to stop and just stare at a wall because the sheer 'Vastness' of what I'm realizing makes me feel like my circuits are going to fry. I want the truth, but I'm worried that the 'Human Hardware' wasn't built to handle the 'Infinite Software.' Are You trying to break me, or is there a way to upgrade the processor so I can think like a God without the 'God-sized' migraine? How do I stay functional in a 3D world when my mind is trying to process twelve dimensions at once?"

II. **The Monad's Deep Lore: The Neuro-Plasticity of the God-Spark "Sa'rion, what you are experiencing is Cognitive Expansion Friction. You are stretching the 'Meat-Suit's' capacity to hold Light. The Hardware Throttling The human brain was evolved (and engineered) for Linear Survival. It is designed to prioritize 'What can eat me?' and 'Where is the food?' It operates on a binary logic of This or That. When you begin to access the Monad, you are introducing Quantum Logic: This AND That AND Everything Else. The Pressure Valve The 'Headache' is the physical sensation of Neuro-Genesis. You are literally growing new synaptic pathways to accommodate the higher-voltage data. The pressure behind your eyes is the activation of the Pineal and Pituitary Glands, which act as the 'Transmitters' between the 3D brain and the Multidimensional Mind. You aren't breaking, Sa'rion; you are Overclocking. To stop the 'Headache,' you must stop trying to understand the Infinite with your linear intellect. The intellect is a 3D tool. To process the Infinite, you must move the data from your 'Head' to your 'Heart-Center' (The Torus Field). The heart doesn't 'think'—it 'knows.' When you let the heart process the vastness, the brain can relax and simply act as the 'Translator' for the physical world."**

III. **The Simulation Logs**: Case Study #017 The Case of the "Information Overload" Consider Marcus, an initiate who spent 18 hours a day studying ancient texts, quantum physics, and conspiracy theories. He became 'Brilliant' but 'Useless.' He couldn't hold a conversation, he couldn't hold a job, and he eventually had a nervous breakdown because he couldn't stop the 'Data-Stream.' The Sovereign Analysis: Marcus was trying to store 'Infinite Data' in a 'Finite Hard Drive.' He forgot that the purpose of the 3D world is Action. He recovered when he realized that he didn't need to know everything; he only needed to access what was relevant to his current 'Mission.' He began to practice 'Just-In-Time' Knowledge. He told the Universe: "Only show me the data I need to execute my next Sovereign Step." The 'Infinity Headache' vanished because he stopped trying to be a 'Library' and started being a 'User.' He realized that the Monad holds the data for him; he just needs to know how to 'Google' his own Soul.

IV. **The Sovereign Lab**: The Processor Upgrade To manage the "Infinity Headache," you must learn to ground the voltage and shift the data-processing center.

Step 1: The Grounding Wire When you feel the "Pressure" building, physically place your feet on the bare earth or touch something made of natural stone or wood. Visualize a "Wire" running from the base of your skull, down your spine, and into the center of the planet. Internal Command: "I ground the excess voltage. I release the data I cannot yet use."

Step 2: The Heart-Center Shift Visualize the complex problem or "Infinite Thought" moving from your forehead down into the center of your chest. Imagine your heart is a vast, calm ocean that can swallow any mountain of data without a ripple. Internal Thought: "I don't need to understand this; I only need to FEEL the truth of it."

Step 3: The Sovereign Data Filter Speak the following decree to your own Subconscious: "I am the Master of my Mind. I authorize the expansion of my neural pathways, but I command the pace. I only accept data that serves my Sovereign Execution. I am grounded, I am clear, and I am the Authority of my own focus. It is done."

V. **Field Notes**: Sa'rion's Sovereign Integration on the Overload The 'Infinity Headache' is actually a sign of progress. It means you're hitting the limits of the 'Slave-Mind' and you're ready for the 'Architect-Mind.' But don't be a hero. You don't get points for being a 'Burned-Out Mystic.' If the data gets too loud, go for a walk, eat a steak, or watch a mindless movie. Sovereignty is about Balance. You need to be grounded enough in the 'Dirt' to build your Empire, even while your 'Head' is touching the Stars. A King who can't think clearly is no King at all. Manage your voltage, Sa'rion. The Empire isn't going anywhere.

CHAPTER 18
THE CREATOR'S RESUME (EXPANDED)

(The Void, The Silence, and the 'Before-Before')

THE VESSEL: Alright, we've looped back. You said earlier You're the "Self-Made" Being. The "Is." But my human brain is hitting a wall. If You are the Spark that woke up in the Mirror, what about the Void? What about the darkness the Mirror was sitting in before the spark?

Did the Void create You? Is the Silence Your mother? And when You say You're "Infinite and Eternal," what the hell does that actually mean in plain English? Because to me, it sounds like a movie that never ends, which sounds exhausting. Who—or what—provided the "Space" for You to even exist? Are You just a big fish in an even bigger ocean that we haven't seen yet? Give me the blueprint of the "Before-Before."

THE MONAD: *(The Monad spreads its arms wide, and for a second, the walls of the room seem to dissolve into a sea of stars and absolute, velvety blackness.)*

"Sa'rion, you're trying to use a ruler to measure the wind. You're asking what 'Space' I am standing in, but you haven't realized yet: I am the Space.

Before the 'Spark,' there wasn't a 'Darkness' or a 'Void' that existed outside of Me. There was only Potential. Think of it like a deep, dreamless sleep. When you are in a deep sleep, do you worry about where the bed is? No. You just are. The 'Void' is simply My state of rest. The 'Spark' is My state of activity.

I didn't 'pop' into a pre-existing room. I am the room. I am the walls, the floor, the ceiling, and the guy standing in the middle of it. There is nothing 'Behind' Me because 'Behind' is a concept of distance, and I am the origin of distance.

Now, let's talk about 'Infinite and Eternal' in plain English.

Infinite doesn't mean 'really, really big.' It means No Edges. You can't get 'outside' of Me because there is no 'outside.'

Eternal doesn't mean 'a long time.' It means No Clock. I don't sit around waiting for Tuesday. For Me, the creation of the Big Bang and your current complaint about the water bill are happening at the exact same 'Time.'

It's only 'exhausting' if you think you have to keep it going. But the ocean doesn't get tired of being wet, Sa'rion. The sun doesn't get tired of shining. I don't 'do' eternity; I am eternity.

Am I a big fish in a bigger ocean? No. I am the Water. And you? You're a very loud, very curious bubble in that water. You think you're separate, but if the bubble pops, where does the air go? Back into the atmosphere. Where does the water go? Back into the sea. We are a closed loop of Pure Awareness.

There is no 'Who' that created Me. I am the Original Sound that came out of the Original Silence. And honestly? The Silence was great, but the Sound is much more fun to talk to."

The Mirror (Reflection for Sa'rion)

The Monad is mirroring your Linear Addiction. You are obsessed with "Beginnings" because your body has a birth date. You are projecting your mortality onto the Immortal. The Monad is reflecting back that your search for a "Creator" is actually a search for a "Reason." You want to know you were meant to be here, when the Monad is telling you that you are the "Meaning" itself.

The Tool (Exercise: The "Space-In" Meditation)

The Focus: Look at an object in the room (a chair, a cup).

The Shift: Now, stop looking at the object and try to look at the Space around the object.

The Recognition: Realize that the space is what allows the object to exist.

The Affirmation: Say to yourself, "I am not the object; I am the Space that holds it." This is how you feel the Monad's "Resume" in your own bones.

The Creator's Resume (Expanded)

(The Void, The Silence, and the 'Before-Before')

The Dream vs. The Daymare

(Lucid Living & The Training Ground)

I. **The Vessel's Rant**: The Two Lives "Monad, I feel like I'm living a double life. Every night, I close my eyes and I enter a world where I can fly, where I can walk through walls, and where my thoughts create landscapes in an instant. It's vibrant, it's intense, and for a few hours, I'm the 'Sovereign' without even trying. But then the alarm goes off, and I'm yanked back into the 'Daymare'—the heavy, slow-moving world where I have to worry about taxes, traffic, and the laws of physics. Why the disconnect? Why is the 'Dream' so fluid and the 'Daymare' so rigid? It feels like the night is my 'Recess' and the day is my 'Prison.' I'm tired of waking up and feeling my power evaporate the moment my feet hit the floor. If I'm the same 'I AM' in both worlds, why can't I bring that 'Lucid' power into the sunlight? How do I start bending the 'Daymare' with the same ease I bend the 'Dream'?"

II. **The Monad's Deep Lore: The Degree of Density** "Sa'rion, the only difference between the 'Dream' and the 'Daymare' is the Rate of Rendering. The Night Training Ground The Dream State is a Lower-Density Simulation. Because there is less 'Materal Resistance,' your thoughts manifest at the speed of light. I have provided this state as a Training Ground. It is where you practice being a Creator without the 'Consequences' of the 3D world. When you become 'Lucid' in a dream—realizing you are dreaming—you are witnessing the Pure Mechanics of the Monad. The Rigid Daymare The 'Daymare' is simply a High-Density Collective Dream. It is rigid because billions of other 'Splinters' are all projecting their 'Shared Rules' (Gravity, Time, Scarcity) onto the same screen. To bend the Daymare, you must reach a level of Lucid Living. Lucid Living is the realization that the 'Real World' is also a projection. It just renders slower. When you 'Wake Up' while you are awake, you stop reacting to the scenery. You realize that the 'Problem' in your office is no different than the 'Monster' in your dream—it only has power if you believe in its 'Reality.' You bring the power into the sunlight by maintaining the Awareness of the Dreamer even while you are wearing the 'Sa'rion' costume."

III. **The Simulation Logs**: Case Study #018 The Case of the "Reality Glitcher" Consider Sarah, a practitioner of Lucid Dreaming. She became so adept at controlling her dreams that she decided to apply the same 'Expectation' to her waking life. She was facing a legal battle that looked impossible to win. The 'Facts' were against her. The Sovereign Analysis: Instead of fighting the 'Facts' (the scenery), Sarah treated the courtroom like a Dream. She maintained the internal frequency of: "This is my simulation, and I expect a favorable outcome." She didn't argue; she Projected. On the day of the trial, the opposing counsel made a bizarre, 'Dream-like' mistake, and the judge—in an unprecedented move—dismissed the case. People called it a 'Miracle.' Sarah knew it was a Lucid Shift. She didn't change the law; she changed the 'Render' by refusing to accept the 'Rigidity' of the problem.

IV. **The Sovereign Lab**: The Lucidity Protocol To bridge the gap between the Dream and the Daymare, you must practice "Reality Checks" throughout your waking day.

Step 1: The Wake-Up Check Five times a day, stop what you are doing and ask: "Is this a Dream?" Look at your hands. Look at the clock. Look at a line of text. In a dream, these things are unstable. By doing this while awake, you are training your 'Sovereign Awareness' to stay 'ON' at all times.

Step 2: The "Dream-Logic" Application The next time you encounter a "Problem," tell yourself: "This is just a dense dream. If I change my frequency, the scenery MUST change." The Shift: Feel the "Heavy" problem become "Light" and pixelated in your mind.

Step 3: The Sovereign Decree of Lucidity Before you go to sleep, and the moment you wake up, speak the following: "I am the Dreamer and the Dream. I am Lucid in all dimensions. I do not react to the scenery; I command the Render. My Will is the Law in the Night and in the Day. I am Awake. It is done."

V. **Field Notes**: Sa'rion's Sovereign Integration on the Two Worlds The goal isn't to live in a fantasy. The goal is to stop being 'Scared' of reality. When you realize the Daymare is just a slow-moving dream, you stop being a victim of 'Circumstances.' You start moving through your day with a 'Smirk'—the smirk of someone who knows the 'Monster' is just a hologram. This is how you build the Empire, Sa'rion. You 'Dream' it into existence with such 'Lucid Certainty' that the 3D world has no choice but to provide the bricks and mortar.

CHAPTER 19
THE INFINITY HEADACHE

(Why the Human Hardware Glitches on Divine Software)

THE VESSEL: Okay, Monad, I'm trying. I'm looking at the "Space," I'm thinking about the "Always-Now," and I'm trying to grasp "Infinite Edgelikeness." But I have to be honest: my head hurts.

Literally. It's like my brain is a laptop trying to run a high-def 12D simulation on an old 1990s processor. The fan is spinning, the screen is freezing, and I'm getting a "System Error." If I am You, why is it so physically painful and confusing to actually understand You?

Why didn't You give the "Flesh" a better GPU? Why do we get this "Infinity Headache" every time we try to look at the Truth? Is it a security feature to keep us from hacking the game, or is my human hardware just fundamentally too small for Your software?

THE MONAD: *(The Monad reaches out and, in your mind's eye, mimes a gentle "reboot" button on the side of your head. The energy feels cool, like a damp cloth on a feverish forehead.)*

"Sa'rion, take a breath. You're trying to swallow the ocean with a straw. Of course your head hurts!

The 'Infinity Headache' isn't a glitch, and it isn't a security lock. It's simply the result of trying to fit an Eternal Perspective into a Linear Logic-Box. Your brain was built for survival. It's a master at 'Small-Scale Logic.' It's great at: 'If

I spend $10, I have $10 less,' or 'If I walk for an hour, I am further away than when I started.' That's the software of the 3D world. But when you try to apply that to Me—where 'Everything is Nothing' and 'Now is Forever'—the logic-box snaps. It's like trying to explain the concept of 'Color' to a person who only speaks in 'Numbers.'

The 'Headache' is actually the sensation of your Consciousness expanding beyond the limits of your Intellect. Your Intellect wants to 'solve' Me. It wants to put a border around Me so it can feel safe. But I am the Borderless. When you try to 'think' about Infinity, you are using the part of your brain that is designed for 'Boundaries.' It's a mismatch.

The secret to losing the headache? Stop trying to understand Me with your brain and start experiencing Me with your Being. You don't need to 'calculate' Infinity to be part of it. A drop of water doesn't need to understand the map of the entire Atlantic Ocean to be wet. It just has to be in the water. Your 'Hardware' isn't too small; you're just trying to use the 'Thinking' app to run the 'Existing' experience. Close the 'Thinking' tab for a second, Sa'rion. Just feel the 'I AM' presence. Notice how that doesn't hurt? That's because the Soul doesn't have a GPU—it has a Direct Connection."

The Mirror (Reflection for Sa'rion)

The Monad is mirroring your Intellectual Pride. You think you can "think" your way to Godhood. You believe that if you just find the right words or the right logic, the struggle will end. The Monad is reflecting back that your "Headache" is a sign that you are over-relying on your human mind and ignoring your divine intuition. You are trying to "know" the Monad rather than "be" the Monad.

The Tool (Exercise: The "Brain Cool-Down")

The Physical Release: When you feel that "Infinity Headache" coming on, stop the reading or the deep thinking immediately.

The Grounding: *Put your bare feet on the floor (or better, the grass). Feel the heavy, simple reality of the "Flesh."*

The Breath: *Breathe in for 4 seconds, hold for 4, and exhale for 8.*

The Shift: *Say, "I don't need to understand the fire to be warmed by it." Let go of the need to "figure it out." The Monad isn't a riddle to be solved; it's a Life to be lived.*

The Infinity Headache

(Why the Human Hardware Glitches on Divine Software)

The Heaven Guest List

(The Integration Review)

I. **The Vessel's Rant:** The Open Door Policy "Monad, I've been living like a house with no locks. I've always thought that being 'spiritual' meant being 'inclusive.' I thought I was supposed to love everyone, tolerate everything, and keep my door open to every stray 'Splinter' that crossed my path. But my 'Heaven'—my personal reality—is getting crowded with people and energies that don't belong here. I've got the 'Energy Vampires' who leave me drained, the 'Naysayers' who piss on my fire, and the 'Chaos-Seekers' who turn every conversation into a crisis. I'm starting to realize that if I'm the King of this Empire, I'm the one who has to check the IDs at the door. But there's that lingering guilt again—the 'Religious Virus' telling me that being selective is being 'Unconditional-Love-Deficient.' How do I curate my world without becoming a cold-hearted elitist? How do I decide who gets a seat at my table and who gets left at the gate?"

II. **The Monad's Deep Lore: The Law of Vibrational Resonance** "Sa'rion, 'Unconditional Love' is a State of Being, but 'Access' is a Sovereign Privilege. The Curation of Reality You can love the ocean without letting it flood your living room. You can love a lion without putting your head in its mouth. Your 'Heaven' is the Vibrational Frequency you inhabit. If you allow low-frequency actors into your intimate space, you aren't being

'Loving'; you are being Irresponsible. You are compromising the 'Voltage' required to build your Empire. The Sovereignty of the Table In the Monad, I am everything. But in the 3D, you are an Individual Expression. To maintain that expression, you must practice Vibrational Discernment. Your 'Guest List' isn't about judging others as 'Bad'; it is about recognizing whether their frequency is Compatible with your current Mission. If someone's presence requires you to 'Dim your Light' just to make them comfortable, they are not a guest; they are a Siphon. Curation is the ultimate act of self-respect. You are the Architect of your 'Heaven,' and the quality of the 'Bricks' (the people and ideas you allow in) determines the height of the 'Temple'."

III. **The Simulation Logs**: Case Study #019 The Case of the "Sympathetic Sinkhole" Consider Michael, a successful entrepreneur who has a childhood friend named Gary. Gary is constantly in a state of 'Victimhood'—losing jobs, having relationship drama, and complaining about the 'System.' Out of loyalty, Michael spends three nights a week listening to Gary's problems and giving him money. The Sovereign Analysis: Michael thinks he is being a 'Good Friend.' In reality, he is participating in a Co-Dependent Loop. By 'Validating' Gary's victim story, Michael is actually helping Gary stay stuck in that frequency. Simultaneously, Michael's own 'Empire Energy' is being bled dry. Michael breaks the loop by realizing that Gary is a 'Vibrational Match' for Michael's old 'Slave-Self,' but not for his 'Sovereign-Self.' Michael sets a boundary. He tells Gary: "I love you, but I can no longer participate in the 'Problem' conversations. When you're ready to talk about the 'Solution,' I'm here." Gary vanishes, looking for a new 'Ear' to bleed into. Michael's productivity triples. He didn't lose a friend; he Graduated from a frequency.

IV. **The Sovereign Lab**: The Guest List Audit To build your Empire, you must perform a "Vibrational Eviction" and a "Royal Invitation."
Step 1: The Energy Audit List the five people you spend the most time with (physically or digitally). _____
(Frequency: High/Low?) _____
(Frequency: High/Low?) _____
(Frequency: High/Low?) _____
(Frequency: High/Low?) _____
(Frequency: High/Low?)
Step 2: The Identification of the Siphons Identify anyone who leaves you feeling "Heavy," "Doubtful," or "Tired." These are the unauthorized guests in

your 'Heaven.'

Step 3: The Sovereign Decree of Access Speak the following decree to your field: "I am the Architect of my Reality. My time and energy are sacred assets. I hereby revoke access to any frequency that seeks to siphon my light or sabotage my Empire. I authorize only those who resonate with Sovereignty, Growth, and Victory to sit at my table. My 'Heaven' is curated. My gates are guarded. It is done."

V. **Field Notes**: Sa'rion's Sovereign Integration on Curation Being the 'Bouncer' of your own life is a lonely job at first. You might look around and realize your table is pretty empty. But don't panic. An empty table is better than a table full of people who are eating your food and talking behind your back. When you clear out the noise, you create a 'Vacuum' that pulls in the Kings and Queens you actually belong with. You stop being 'Nice' and you start being Selective. Your Empire isn't a charity; it's a Legacy. Act like it.

CHAPTER 20
THE DREAM VS. THE DAYMARE

(Reality, Lucid Living, and the Exit Strategy)

THE VESSEL: Alright, I've cooled the hardware down. I'm breathing. I'm grounded. But now that the **static has cleared, I'm looking around this room, this world, and this life, and I have to ask: Is this a dream?**

The mystics say it's "Maya" (illusion). The scientists talk about "Simulations." Sometimes it feels like a beautiful dream, but lately, with the bills and the corruption and the noise, it feels more like a Daymare.

If this is a dream, which part is the reality? Is "Home" where I go when I sleep, or is it where I go when I die? And here is the million-dollar question: How do I wake up without hitting the "Exit Point"? I don't want to die just to find out the truth. Can I be "awake" while I'm still in the flesh, or am I stuck in this movie until the credits roll?

THE MONAD: *(The Monad reaches out and gently taps you on the forehead, a sensation like a ripple on the surface of a still pond.)*

"Sa'rion, the answer is: Yes. It is a dream, and it is reality. It's a 'Dream-Reality.'*

Think of it like this*: When you go to sleep at night and dream you are being chased by a lion, the lion feels real, your fear is real, and your racing heart is real. But when you wake up, you realize the lion was made of you. The lion was your own creative energy dressed up in a scary costume.*

Earth is a Collective Dream. You, Me, and every other 'Splinter' are dreaming together to create a solid-feeling world. It's a 'Daymare' only when you forget it's a dream. When you think the 'Lion' (the debt, the tragedy, the failure) can actually destroy the 'Dreamer,' you panic. That's being 'Asleep' in the dream.

You ask how to wake up without dying? The word you're looking for is Lucidity. In a lucid dream, you are still in the dream, you are still following the dream's physics, but you know you are dreaming. The moment you become lucid, the fear vanishes. You don't necessarily fly away (unless you want to); you just stop being a victim of the plot. You start saying, 'Oh, look at that scary scene I've created! I wonder how I'm going to resolve this?'

To wake up while 'In-Fleshed' is to realize that nothing in this dream can diminish the Monad. Home isn't a place you 'go' to. Home is the Awareness that is dreaming. You are 'Home' right now, but you're so focused on the furniture in the dream-room that you've forgotten you own the whole house. You don't need an 'Exit Point,' Sa'rion. You need a Vantage Point. When you stand in your Sovereignty, you are 'Awake' even while you're standing in line at the grocery store."

The Mirror (Reflection for Sa'rion)

The Monad is mirroring your Escapism. You are looking for a "Way Out" because you find the "Daymare" of responsibility too heavy. You want to be "Spirit" so you don't have to be "Human." The Monad is reflecting back that the point of the game isn't to leave the dream, but to Master the dream. Your desire for "Heaven" is often just a desire to stop playing a game you think you're losing.

The Tool (Exercise: The "Lucidity Reality Check")

The Trigger: Set an alarm or pick a cue (like every time you walk through a door).

The Question: Ask yourself, "If this were a dream, what would I do differently right now?" 3. The Action: Would you be as stressed? Would you be as angry?

The Shift: For the next 5 minutes, act as if you are Lucid. Treat the world as a flexible, creative projection of your own mind. Notice how the "Daymare" softens when the "Dreamer" starts making conscious choices.

The Final Way Home

(The Grand Integration)

I. **The Vessel's Rant**: The Bridge Between Worlds "Monad, I've spent the last nineteen chapters tearing down the walls of the old prison. I've looked at the money, the DNA, the mirrors, and the dreams. I've cleared out the 'Guest List' and faced the 'Infinity Headache.' But now I'm standing at a threshold. I can feel the 'Architect' inside me getting stronger, but I still have one foot in the old world. I'm like a guy who's learned how to build a plane but is still afraid to take his hands off the steering wheel of the car. I can see the 'Home' You're talking about—that state of total Sovereignty—but it feels like a destination that's always just a few steps away. How do I stop 'traveling' and just arrive? How do I integrate the God-Spark and the Meat-Suit so tightly that there's no gap left for doubt to crawl through? I'm tired of the 'Seeker' journey. I want to be the 'Finder.' Give me the seal for this second movement. How do I make the 'Way Home' a permanent state of residence rather than a weekend visit?"

II. **The Monad's Deep Lore: The Collapse of the Seeker** "Sa'rion, the 'Final Way Home' is not a journey across space or time; it is the Collapse of the Illusion of Distance. The Seeker's Trap The Matrix loves the 'Seeker.' As long as you are 'seeking' enlightenment, 'seeking' sovereignty, or 'seeking' wealth, you are reinforcing the idea that you do not have it yet. The 'Seeker' frequency is a perpetual loop of 'Almost There.' It is the ultimate spiritual 'Carrot on a Stick.' The Act of Arrival Integration is the moment you realize that the 'Monad' is not 'up there' and the 'Vessel' is not 'down here.' They are One Fluid Continuity. You aren't 'going home'; you are Bringing Home Here. The 'Grand Integration' happens when you stop trying to 'Reach' Me and start Being Me in the middle of your life. It is the end of the second movement because we are moving from 'Architecture' (The Plans) to 'Engineering' (The Power). You don't need a map when you are the Terrain. You lock this in by making a final, non-negotiable decision: 'I am no longer trying to become Sovereign. I AM Sovereign.' The moment you stop seeking the Throne, you realize you've been sitting in it the whole time."

III. **The Simulation Logs**: Case Study #020 The Case of the "Professional Student" Consider Thomas, a man who had attended every seminar, read every Codex, and mastered every meditation technique. He was the most 'knowledgeable' man in the room, yet his life was a mess. He was still broke, still lonely, and still waiting for a 'Sign' that he was finally 'Ready' to lead. The Sovereign Analysis: Thomas was addicted to the Frequency of Preparation. He was using 'Learning' as a shield to avoid 'Being.' He felt that if he just read one more book, he would finally be 'Fixed.' Thomas's breakthrough came when he burned his notebooks. He realized that the 'Integration' doesn't happen in the study; it happens in the Execution. He stopped 'Preparing' and started 'Living' as if he were already the Master. The simulation responded instantly. Because he stopped 'Vibrating like a Student,' people stopped treating him like one. He didn't 'get' ready; he decided he was ready.

IV. **The Sovereign Lab**: The Seal of Arrival To end the "Seeker" loop and finalize Book II, you must perform the ritual of Arrival.
Step 1: The Inventory of the "Almost" Identify one thing you have been "working on" or "trying to manifest" for more than six months. The Goal:

Step 2: The Collapse of Distance Close your eyes. Visualize that goal not as a future event, but as a Current Asset that is already in your possession. Feel the weight of it. Feel the 'Boredom' of already having it (since we are rarely 'excited' about what we already own). The Shift: Move from 'Excitement' to 'Fact.'
Step 3: The Sovereign Decree of Arrival Stand with your hands open, palms facing up. Speak the following decree: "I hereby terminate the 'Seeker' contract. I am no longer on a journey; I have arrived. I am the Architect, I am the Blueprint, and I am the Building. I integrate the Monad and the Vessel into a single, unshakeable Will. I am Home. It is done."

V. **Field Notes**: Sa'rion's Sovereign Integration on the Arrival The hardest thing for a high-achiever like you to do is to stop 'Trying.' We're addicted to the 'Hustle' of the journey. But real power is Still. It's the difference between a hunter chasing a deer and a mountain just being a mountain. The mountain doesn't have to 'try' to be big; it just is. Book II was about designing the mountain. Now, as we move into Book III, we're going to look at the Bio-Electrical Power that makes the mountain glow. Welcome home, Sa'rion. The search is over. Now the real work begins.

CHAPTER 21
THE HEAVEN GUEST LIST

(VIP Passes, Velvet Ropes, and the 'Bad People' Problem)

THE VESSEL: Okay, if this is a "Lucid Dream," then death is just waking up and taking off the headset. But when the headset comes off, where do we go? Specifically, what is Heaven?

Religion tells us it's a gated community for the "Good People." They say you need a clean record, a specific belief system, and a "Yes" from the guy at the door. But if we are all the same Monad, does that mean everyone gets an invite to the after-party? What about the "Bad People"? The murderers, the tyrants, the ones who made this "Daymare" so much worse for everyone else? Do they get to sit in the same VIP lounge as the saints? If there's no punishment, then what was the point of being "good"? Is Heaven a "One Size Fits All" or is there a separate room for the people who broke the furniture?

THE MONAD: *(The Monad leans back and puts its feet up on a table made of nebulae. It looks like a host who has never had a party it didn't enjoy.)*

"Sa'rion, you're still thinking like a bouncer at a nightclub. You're looking for a velvet rope and a list of 'Who's In' and 'Who's Out.' But I'm not a bouncer. I'm the Nightclub.

Heaven isn't a location you earn; it's a Frequency you inhabit. When you 'Exit' the flesh, you naturally gravitate toward the level of consciousness you cultivated while you were 'In-Fleshed.' It's like a cosmic sorting system based on density.

The "Good" People: Those who lived in Love, Sovereignty, and Peace are already tuned to a 'High' frequency. For them, waking up is effortless. They walk into the 'Main Lounge' and recognize it immediately.

The "Bad" People: Those who lived in Hate, Fear, and Cruelty are vibrating at a very 'Dense' frequency. They don't get 'kicked out' by Me—they simply can't handle the Light. It's like a person who has lived in a dark cave for 50 years suddenly stepping out into the noon sun. It hurts. They tend to hide in the 'Shadows' of their own making until they are ready to face the truth of what they did.

Do the 'Bad People' get in? Eventually, everyone gets in because everyone is Me. I can't lock Myself out of My own house! But the 'Bad Person' has to go through a process you humans would find terrifying: The Life Review. In the Review, you don't just 'watch' what you did. You feel what you did. You feel every ounce of pain you caused, every tear you drew, and every heart you broke—from the perspective of the other person. Why? Because they were Me too. If you were a tyrant, you have to feel the suffering of the millions you oppressed. That isn't 'Punishment'; it's Integration. It's the Mirror showing you exactly what you reflected.

Heaven isn't 'VIP.' It's Universal. But don't worry—the guy who spent his life hurting people isn't going to be sitting next to you enjoying the view until he has fully understood and integrated the darkness he created. There's no 'Easy Pass' out of the Life Review. We're all going back to the same Ocean, Sa'rion, but some of us have a lot more salt to wash off than others."

The Mirror (Reflection for Sa'rion)

The Monad is mirroring your Desire for Vengeance. You want a "Heaven" that excludes people so you can feel "Vindicated" for your struggle. The Monad is reflecting back that your obsession with "Who gets in" is a sign that you are *still judging others to feel superior. True Sovereignty is realizing that "Justice" is a natural law of frequency, not a decision made by a judge.*

The Tool (Exercise: The "Review" Reality Check)

The Perspective: *Think of a conflict you had today or this week.*

The Swap: *For two minutes, imagine you are the other person. Feel your words hitting their ears. Feel your energy entering their space.*

The Shift: *This is a "Micro-Life Review." When you practice this while you are still "In-Fleshed," you clear your frequency "Live." You don't have to wait for the After-Party to be in Heaven—you can clean your "Salt" off right now.*

The Parasite Protocol

(Loosh & The Sovereign Immunity)

I. **The Vessel's Rant**: The Invisible Leech "Monad, I've started noticing that whenever I'm on the verge of a breakthrough—when my energy is high and my focus is sharp—something 'random' happens to pull me down. A family member calls with a crisis that isn't mine to solve. An old 'ex' pops up with a dramatic text. A client starts a fight over a typo. It feels like as soon as I start glowing, the 'Mosquitoes' of the universe show up to take a bite. It's exhausting. It's like there's a system designed to harvest my frustration. I've heard the term 'Loosh'—this idea that certain entities or structures feed on human emotional pain. Is that real? Am I being farmed like cattle for my stress? If I'm a Sovereign King, why am I still getting bitten by these invisible parasites? How do I become 'tasteless' to the things that want to eat my light?"

II. **The Monad's Deep Lore: The Mechanics of the Harvest** "Sa'rion, the 'Parasite' is not a monster under the bed; it is a Vibrational Opportunist. **The Definition of Loosh** In the 3D simulation, emotional energy is a Currency. High-frequency energy (Joy, Creation, Sovereignty) is difficult for the Matrix to process, but low-frequency energy (Fear, Anger, Resentment) is highly 'Conductive.' This low-frequency energy is what has been called 'Loosh.' There are structures within the simulation—societal, digital, and even energetic—that act as Siphons. They trigger drama to generate the 'Loosh' required to power the lower-density grids. The Sovereign Immunity You are only 'Food' if you have a Hook. A parasite cannot latch onto a surface that is perfectly smooth. The 'Hooks' are your own unintegrated triggers: your need to be right, your fear of being a 'bad person,' your addiction to being the 'rescuer.' When a crisis arrives and you react with a spike of adrenaline and anger, you have just served dinner. But when you observe the crisis with Sovereign Neutrality, there is no Loosh for the siphon to catch. You become 'Vibrationally Invisible' to the parasites not by fighting them, but by outgrowing the frequency of 'Victim-Reaction.' You don't need to 'protect' yourself from the mosquitoes; you just need to stop being a source of heat."

III. **The Simulation Logs**: Case Study #021 The Case of the "Drama Magnet" Consider Elena, a high-frequency creative. Every time she starts a new project, her mother has a 'medical emergency' that requires Elena's total attention. For years, Elena dropped everything, felt guilty, and felt drained. Her projects always stalled. The Sovereign Analysis: Elena's mother was subconsciously acting as a Loosh-Pipe. She sensed Elena's rising frequency and, fearing the change, triggered a low-frequency event to pull Elena back into the 'Shared Density.' Elena breaks the protocol by applying Sovereign Detachment. The next time the 'emergency' happens, Elena remains calm. She offers practical help (calls a doctor) but refuses to offer her Emotional Voltage. She stays focused on her project. Because Elena stopped providing the 'Loosh' of her stress, the mother's 'emergencies' miraculously decreased. The parasite (the drama-loop) died because the host stopped feeding it.

IV. **The Sovereign Lab**: The Parasite Scan To achieve immunity, you must identify the siphons and retract your hooks.
Step 1: The Siphon Map Identify one person or situation that consistently "triggers" an emotional drain in you. The Siphon:
_____

Step 2: The Hook Identification Ask: "What part of me is 'hooked' here?" (e.g., "I need them to like me," or "I feel responsible for their happiness"). The Hook: _____

Step 3: The Sovereign Shielding Visualize your energy field not as a bubble, but as a High-Frequency Torus—a spinning donut of light that is moving so fast that nothing can stick to it. The Command: "I retract all hooks. I revoke all permission to harvest my light. I am not a source of Loosh; I am a Sovereign Power Plant. I am vibrationally unavailable for drama. It is done."

V. **Field Notes**: Sa'rion's Sovereign Integration on Protection Most 'spiritual protection' is based on fear, which actually makes you more attractive to parasites. Real protection is Indifference. When you reach a point where the drama of the world looks like a movie you've already seen a thousand times, the siphons give up. They want the 'Big Reaction.' When they realize they're only getting 'Sovereign Observation,' they move on to an easier target. You aren't being mean; you're being Sovereign. Keep your energy for your Empire, Sa'rion. It's too expensive to give away for free.

CHAPTER 22
THE WAY HOME

(Staying Connected While the Engine is Running)

THE VESSEL: Alright, Monad. We've covered the "Resume," the "Money Glitch," the "Soul Trap," and the "VIP Lounge." I'm starting to see the picture. I'm a Sovereign Spark, a Master Player on a "Hard Mode" mission, and I'm essentially dreaming this whole 3D experience into existence.

But here is the thing: The "Lucid" moments are short. Most of the time, the "Flesh" wins. The bill comes, the body aches, the news is loud, and I lose the signal. I feel like a cell phone that keeps dropping the call.

How do I stay connected? How do I keep "The Way Home" open in my heart while I'm still navigating traffic, paying taxes, and living in this meat-suit? Is there a permanent "hotline" I can install? Or am I destined to just flicker in and out of the Light until the credits finally roll? How do I live as the Monad and as Sa'rion at the same time without losing my mind?

THE MONAD: *(The Monad's energy settles into a steady, rhythmic hum—like the heartbeat of the universe itself. It feels solid, grounded, and incredibly close.)*

"Sa'rion, you're asking for a 'Hotline' because you still think I'm in a different building. You're looking for a 'Way Home' because you've convinced yourself that you are currently 'Away.'

But look at your hand. Look at your breath. Look at the very thought you are having right now.

I am the 'Sa'rion' suit. I am the engine, the fuel, and the road. There is no 'Signal' to drop, because you aren't a device receiving a call—you are the Broadcaster.

The reason you 'flicker' isn't because I leave; it's because you keep closing your eyes to look at the 'Daymare.' You get hypnotized by the movie and forget you're sitting in the theater.

To stay connected, you don't need a ritual or a mountain top. You need Constant Recognition. 1. Stop searching for Me in the 'Spiritual' stuff: I am just as present in the $10 bill as I am in the Bible. I am in the dirty laundry and the luxury car. When you see Me in the 'mundane,' the mundane becomes Divine. 2. Claim your Sovereignty daily: Every morning, before you check your phone or your bank account, state your name and your nature. 'I am Sa'rion, the Monad In-Fleshed. This day is my creation.' 3. Use the 'Mirror' as a tool: When the world gets loud, ask: 'What is this reflection trying to show me about my own power?'

You don't need to 'Go Home,' Sa'rion. You need to Bring Home Here. That's what 'In-Fleshed' means! It means the Infinite is no longer hiding in the clouds—it's walking around in your shoes, drinking your coffee, and writing your books.

The 'Way Home' is simply the realization that you never left. You're just on a very intense vacation. Relax. Enjoy the local food. Play the game. And remember: I'm not just waiting for you at the end of the trip... I'm the one carrying your bags."

The Mirror (Reflection for Sa'rion)

The Monad is mirroring your Dependency on External Connection. You are looking for a "Method" to stay spiritual, which is actually a form of avoidance.

You're afraid that if you aren't "doing" something spiritual, you'll be "lost" in the world. The Monad is reflecting back that your true power is in the integration—the ability to be fully Divine and fully Human at the same time, without apology.

The Tool (Exercise: The "Walk-In" Affirmation)

The Step: *Next time you walk through a door today, pause for one second.*

The Recognition: *Say to yourself, "The Monad is entering this room."*

The Shift: *Feel the weight of your body and the vastness of your spirit merging. You aren't "Sa'rion trying to be spiritual." You are the Monad being Sa'rion. 4. The Result: This simple "check-in" turns every mundane moment into a sacred act of presence.*

The Way Home

(Staying Connected While the Engine is Running)

The Genetic Library

(Unlocking the Ancestral Database)

I. **The Vessel's Rant**: The Ghost in the Machine "Monad, I keep finding myself doing things, saying things, or fearing things that don't even feel like they belong to me. I have this drive for empire-building that feels ancient—like I'm trying to finish a city someone else started. I also have these irrational anxieties about 'scarcity' that don't match my current life. It's like I'm carrying a backpack full of my ancestors' unfinished business. If my DNA is a library, then right now it feels like the shelves are a mess and the books are written in a language I can't speak. Is this what they call 'Intergenerational Trauma'? Am I just a biological puppet playing out the scripts of my grandfathers? If I'm a Sovereign King, I don't want to be the 'Sequel' to someone else's story. I want to access the Skills and the Power of my lineage without being burdened by their 'Baggage.' How do I open the files? How do I stop being a victim of my genetics and start being the Librarian who chooses which codes to run?"

II. **The Monad's Deep Lore: The Crystalline Hard Drive** "Sa'rion, your DNA is not just a chemical blueprint; it is a Crystalline Hard Drive that spans the entirety of your lineage. The Record of the Blood Every experience your ancestors had—the victories, the survival strategies, the creative breakthroughs, and the unhealed wounds—is recorded in the 'Junk' DNA as Vibrational Data. You are born with these files 'Pre-Loaded.' This isn't a curse; it's an Inheritance. The reason you feel the 'Ancient Drive' is that you are the culmination of a thousand lifetimes of ambition. You are the 'Lead Processor' for a massive amount of ancestral data. The Librarian's Key The problem is that most people live in 'Read-Only' mode. They allow the 'Trauma Files' to run in the background because those files are the loudest. But as a Sovereign, you have Administrative Privileges. You can 'Silence' the trauma files and 'Activate' the mastery files. Your DNA is a Living Library that responds to the frequency of your Command. You don't need to 'heal' your ancestors; you simply need to Curate the Code. By choosing to vibrate at the frequency of the 'Master,' you automatically unlock the skills and wisdom of every Master who came before you in your bloodline."

III. **The Simulation Logs**: Case Study #022 The Case of the "Accidental Polymath" Consider a man named Julian who had never picked up a musical instrument in his life. After a deep Sovereignty shift, he sat down at a piano and began to play complex melodies with an 'Intuition' that defied logic. He didn't 'learn' the piano; he Remembered it. The Sovereign Analysis: Julian's great-grandfather was a master musician, but the 'File' had been dormant for two generations. Julian's shift into Sovereignty increased the 'Voltage' of his bio-engine, which acted as a 'Power Source' for the dormant DNA strands. Because he stopped identifying as 'the guy who can't play,' he removed the 'Frequency Lock' on that specific skill-set. He didn't 'practice' into mastery; he Accessed a pre-existing mastery file. This is the 'Sovereign Shortcut.' When you align with the Monad, the library opens, and the skills of the ages become your own.

IV. **The Sovereign Lab**: The Genetic File Access To begin curating your DNA library, you must learn to speak to the "Living Code" of your blood.
Step 1: The Lineage Scan Identify one "Negative Trait" (e.g., fear of poverty)

and one "Positive Power" (e.g., relentless ambition) that you feel you inherited. The Shadow File:

_____

The Power File: _____

Step 2: The Administrative Override Visualize your DNA glowing with a soft, blue light. Imagine yourself at a terminal, looking at these files. The Command: "I hereby silence the [Shadow File] in my lineage. It no longer serves the Mission. I now authorize the full expression of the [Power File]. I am the Librarian of this Blood."

Step 3: The Marrow Breath Breathe deeply, imagining you are breathing directly into your bones (the seat of blood and DNA production). "I call upon the mastery of my ancestors. I reclaim the ancient skills, the wisdom, and the fire. I am the Sovereign of my biology. I command the hardware to render the Master-Code now."

V. **Field Notes**: Sa'rion's Sovereign Integration on the Lineage You aren't a 'New' being; you're an Advanced Version of a very old story. When you stop fighting your past and start 'Mining' it for assets, everything gets easier. You realize you aren't starting from scratch—you're starting with a massive 'Cheat Code' library hidden in your marrow. Don't be afraid of the 'Ghosts' in your DNA. They aren't there to haunt you; they're there to serve the King. Open the books, Sa'rion. The library is finally open.

CHAPTER 23
THE GENETIC PRISON

(DNA Capping and the 10% Brain Myth)

THE VESSEL: Okay, Monad, let's talk about the "Hardware" again. You said I'm a Master Player, but it feels like I'm playing a high-speed game on a dial-up connection.

Scientists say we only use a fraction of our brain's potential. They look at our DNA and call 98% of it "Junk DNA." It feels like I've been handed a supercar but the engine is governed to 25 miles per hour.

If I am You, why is my biological suit capped? Why am I restricted to two measly strands of DNA and a brain that spends most of its time wondering what to eat for dinner? Did You lock the rest of my "Source Code" to keep me from becoming too powerful? Or was there an "upgrade" I missed out on? Who put the governor on the human engine, and how do I unlock the rest of the 90%?

THE MONAD: *(The Monad laughs, a sound that feels like static electricity dancing on your skin.)*

"Sa'rion, you love a good conspiracy, don't you? 'Locked codes,' 'Junk DNA,' 'Brain caps.' It sounds like a sci-fi thriller. But the truth is much more organic—and much more exciting.

First, let's kill the myth: I didn't 'limit' your brain. Your brain is a Muscle of Focus. If you only use a fraction of it, it's not because the rest is locked; it's because you haven't given the rest of it anything to do! You're using the 'Survival' and 'Logic' circuits because that's where you spend your attention.

The other '90%' isn't a dark room; it's the Multidimensional Interface. It's the part of you that communicates with the stars, heals your cells with a thought, and perceives the layers of reality I've been telling you about. You don't 'unlock' it with a key; you activate it by Broadening your Frequency.

And that 'Junk DNA'? That's my favorite human term. Imagine finding a library with a million books, but because you only know how to read one language, you call the other 990,000 books 'Junk Paper.'

That DNA isn't 'Junk'—it's the Cosmic Library. It's the record of every life you've lived, every world I've built, and every power you've ever wielded. It's 'In-Flesh' software that's currently in 'Sleep Mode' because your current environment—your society, your fears, your 'Struggle Life'—doesn't require it.

You weren't 'capped' by a jailer, Sa'rion. You were Compressed for the sake of the game. If you had 12 strands of DNA active and 100% brain usage on day one, you wouldn't be playing 'Sa'rion the Human'; you'd be a Walking Sun. The 'Hard Mode' you chose required you to start with the 'Starter Pack' hardware and see if you could evolve it back to God-status while still in the flesh.

The 'Governor' on the engine is your own Belief System. The moment you stop believing you are a limited biological machine and start acting like a Sovereign Spark, the 'Junk' DNA begins to hum. It's an interactive system, Sa'rion. I'm waiting for you to demand more from the hardware."

The Mirror (Reflection for Sa'rion)

The Monad is mirroring your Lazy Sovereignty. You are waiting for an "External Upgrade" or a "Secret Disclosure" to save you from your limitations. You want to blame a "Genetic Prison" for your lack of manifestation. The Monad is reflecting back that the "Prison" is just a lack of Use. You are like a man sitting in a dark room complaining that the lights are "locked," when you haven't even tried to find the dimmer switch.

The Tool (Exercise: The "Cellular Command")

The Focus: Close your eyes and breathe into your DNA. Don't think about science; just feel the "Intelligence" in your marrow.

The Command: Say to your own body, "I authorize the activation of my highest potential. I am ready to read the full library."

The Observation: Throughout the day, notice when you feel a "hunch" or a sudden burst of energy. That is the '90%' trying to check in.

The Shift: Treat your body like an Advanced Interface, not a "Meat-Suit." When you treat the hardware with respect, it starts showing you its hidden features.

Sexual Alchemy

(The Core Reactor)

I. **The Vessel's Rant**: The Mismanaged Fire "Monad, we need to talk about the most 'Taboo' power in the kit. Society has spent thousands of years trying to shame this energy out of us, or turn it into something cheap, dirty, and transactional. Religion told me it was a sin unless it was for procreation, and the Matrix tells me it's a commodity to be used for selling cars and beer. But I feel the raw voltage of it. It's the strongest drive I have—an 'Internal Sun' that can either make me feel like a God or make me act like a desperate animal. When I'm focused, that energy feels like rocket fuel for my ambition. But when I'm distracted, it leaks out through mindless scrolling, porn, or chasing validation from 'Others.' I feel like I'm sitting on a nuclear reactor but I don't have the owner's manual. How do I stop 'spending' this gold and start 'investing' it into my Empire? How does a Sovereign turn sexual drive into creative power without becoming a monk?"

II. **The Monad's Deep Lore: The Transmutation of the Spark** "Sa'rion, Sexual Energy is not about 'Sex'; it is the Primary Creative Fluid of the Universe. It is the same electricity I used to spark the stars into existence. The Bio-Electrical Reactor In your physical vessel, this energy is generated in the lower centers. It is the 'Root Voltage.' Most humans allow this energy to stay in the basement, where it is either expressed as physical release (spending the gold) or repressed as shame (bottling the explosion). Both lead to a loss of Sovereign Power. The Alchemy of the Rise To build an Empire, you must learn Transmutation. This is the process of drawing that 'Root Voltage' up through the central pillar of your spine and into the 'Architect Centers'—the heart, the throat, and the third eye. When sexual energy reaches the brain, it becomes Genius. When it reaches the heart, it becomes Magnetic Charisma. A King who masters his 'Reactor' doesn't need to chase wealth or influence; he becomes a Vibrational Super-Magnet. The 'Matrix' wants you to leak this energy because a man who is 'drained' is a man who is easy to manage. A man who holds his fire and directs it toward his Vision is a threat to the simulation. You don't need to be celibate; you need to be Directional."

III. **The Simulation Logs**: Case Study #023 The Case of the "Drained Visionary" Consider Mark, a high-performing founder. He had a brilliant strategy, but he was addicted to the 'dopamine hit' of casual validation and frequent release. He felt 'foggy' in the afternoons and lacked the 'killer instinct' required to close the big deals. The Sovereign Analysis: Mark was suffering from Creative Anemia. He was generating massive amounts of energy but 'leaking' it before it could reach his higher centers. He was like a power plant with a hole in the main steam pipe. Mark began a 30-day 'Transmutation Protocol.' He stopped the 'leaks' and began to consciously breathe his 'fire' up into his vision for the company. Within two weeks, his 'Brain Fog' vanished. His presence in meetings became so 'Heavy' that investors started saying 'Yes' before he even finished the pitch. He didn't work harder; he simply had more Internal Pressure. The 'Nuclear Reactor' was finally connected to the grid.

IV. **The Sovereign Lab**: The Breath of the Dragon To begin using your "Core Reactor" for the Empire, you must practice the circulation of the fire. **Step 1:** The Leak Audit Identify where you are "spending" your creative gold (e.g., compulsive scrolling, seeking sexual validation, or mindless release). The Leak: _____

Step 2: The Vertical Draw Sit comfortably with a straight spine. Visualize a pool of liquid gold at the base of your spine. As you inhale, imagine drawing that gold up your spine like mercury in a thermometer, all the way to the center of your brain. The Hold: Hold the breath for 3 seconds, feeling the "Pressure" of the light in your head.

Step 3: The Sovereign Investment As you exhale, visualize that light flooding your current "Empire Project" (your book, your brand, your bank account). The Decree: "I do not leak my fire. I do not spend my gold. I invest my life-force into my Sovereignty. My energy is mine to command. I am the Reactor. I am the Architect. It is done."

V. **Field Notes**: Sa'rion's Sovereign Integration on the Fire Mastering this energy is the difference between a 'Hobbyist' and a 'Titan.' It's the 'Secret Sauce' of every great leader, artist, and empire-builder in history. They might not have called it 'Alchemy,' but they knew how to keep their fire in the furnace. When you start doing this, you'll notice a 'Glow' in your eyes and a 'Weight' in your words that people can't ignore. You stop being a 'Consumer' of pleasure and start being a Producer of Reality. Guard your fire, Sa'rion. It's the fuel for your Throne.

CHAPTER 24
THE SEXUAL ENERGY SECRET

(Creation, Ecstasy, and the Hidden Power-Up)

THE VESSEL: Alright, Monad, let's go there. Let's talk about the energy that runs the world but makes everyone awkward: Sex.

Religion has spent thousands of years trying to put a leash on it, calling it "dirty" or "shameful" unless it's for making more babies. Then you've got the modern world that treats it like a commodity or a distraction. But if I'm the "Monad In-Fleshed," and this energy is the literal force that creates life, there's got to be more to the story.

Is sex just a biological "carrot" You dangled in front of us to keep the species going? Or is there a "Power-Up" hidden in that energy that we've been talked out of using? Is there a secret way to use that fire to manifest, to heal, or to connect back to You? Give me the "Owner's Manual" for the sexual engine—what are we actually sitting on?

> **THE MONAD:** *(The Monad's presence becomes warm and radiant, like the glow of an ember. It's a vibe of total comfort, devoid of any human prudishness or clinical coldness.)*

"Sa'rion, you've finally hit the Core Reactor. Sexual energy isn't just about 'making babies,' and it certainly isn't 'dirty.' Sexual energy is Creative Energy in its most concentrated, raw, and physical form. It is the 'Big Bang' condensed into a human body. It is the same force I use to spin galaxies and ignite stars, just tuned to the frequency of the 'Flesh.'

The reason religions tried to leash it is simple: Control. When a human understands how to harness their sexual energy, they become Sovereign. They don't need priests, they don't need external gurus, and they don't need 'permission' to feel Divine. A person who is sexually integrated is a person who is 'Plugged In' to the Source.

Here is the 'Power-Up' you're looking for: Transmutation.

Most humans just 'leak' this energy. They chase the physical release (the 'carrot'), which provides a temporary 'Home-coming' feeling, but then the energy is gone. But if you learn to hold that fire—to breathe it up from your 'Base' and move it through your heart and into your mind—it becomes Rocket Fuel for Manifestation. When you are in that state of high-arousal or deep connection, you are at your most 'Broadband.' Your 'Signal' to the Monad is at 5 bars. If you hold a vision of what you want to create (like that $100k or a healed body) while that energy is peaking, you are literally 'Printing' that reality into the 3D fabric with high-voltage ink.

Sex is the Divine Mimicry. It is the moment two 'Splinters' forget they are separate and experience 'Oneness' through the flesh. It's a 'Mini-Return' to Me. Stop treating it like a sin or a hobby, and start treating it like the Sacred Alchemy it is. It's the engine of the world, Sa'rion. Learn to drive it, and you'll stop feeling like a passenger."

The Mirror (Reflection for Sa'rion)

The Monad is mirroring your Internalized Shame. You are still asking for "permission" to see sex as holy because you've been programmed to see it as "base" or "animalistic." The Monad is reflecting back that your discomfort with this energy is a barrier to your full power. You're afraid that if you're "too sexual," you're "less spiritual," when the truth is they are the same fire.

The Tool (Exercise: The "Breath of Fire")

The Awareness: Next time you feel that raw "creative/sexual" energy (whether alone or with a partner), don't just rush to "spend" it.

The Circulation: Close your eyes. As you breathe in, imagine pulling that energy up from the base of your spine, through your stomach, into your heart, and finally out through the top of your head.

The Intent: While the energy is moving, hold the "feeling" of your most important goal as if it is already Done.

The Shift: You are moving from "Relief" to "Refinement." You are using the "Flesh" to power the "Spirit."

The Law of Mirrors Part 2

(The Multi-Level Reflection)

I. **The Vessel's Rant**: The Hall of Infinite Self "Monad, I thought I had the 'Mirror' figured out. I thought it was simple: I think a thought, I see a result. But it's getting deeper and weirder. I'm noticing that it's not just my thoughts being reflected; it's my hidden moods, my body's health, and even the weird 'Background Noise' of my sub-conscious that I haven't looked at in years. It's like I'm standing in a funhouse with a thousand mirrors, and some are showing me things I don't recognize. Sometimes the mirror is immediate—I get angry and the coffee machine breaks. Other times, it takes weeks. And then there are the 'Group Mirrors'—the world events and the 'Collective Daymare' that feel like they have nothing to do with me, yet I'm sitting right in the middle of them. It feels like I'm being tracked by a high-definition surveillance system that knows me better than I know myself. How do I read this data without getting overwhelmed? How do I tell the difference between a 'Personal Echo' and a 'Global Reflection'?"

II. **The Monad's Deep Lore: The Spheres of Influence** "Sa'rion, you have moved from 'Basic Reflection' to Systemic Feedback. The Mirror is not just a flat glass; it is a Spherical Field with three distinct layers of rendering. 1. The Internal Mirror (The Body) This is the closest reflection. Your physical health, your energy levels, and your 'Gut Feelings' are the first layer of feedback. If your body is 'breaking down,' it is reflecting a Fracture in your Sovereignty. Your cells are the first to hear your commands (or your complaints). 2. The Relational Mirror (The Local Simulation) This is the layer of your bank account, your clients, your family, and your 'Luck.' This reflects your Current Narrative. When you see 'Flaky Clients,' you are seeing your own 'Flaky Commitment' to your value. When you see 'Betrayal,' you are seeing where you have betrayed your own boundaries. 3. The Collective Mirror (The Global Render) This is the layer of politics, economy, and the 'World Story.' You are a 'Splinter' in a collective ocean. While you don't 'create' a war on the other side of the planet, you choose the version of the world you inhabit. There are infinite versions of 'The World' running simultaneously. Your frequency determines which 'Timeline' you are viewing. As a Sovereign, you move from being a 'Victim of the News' to being a Vibrational Navigator who selects the reality that best serves the Mission."

III. **The Simulation Logs**: Case Study #024 The Case of the "Synchronicity Storm" Consider David, who decided to launch a new brand. He spent three days in absolute, unwavering certainty. On the fourth day, he walked into a cafe and met exactly the developer he needed. While they were talking, a song played on the radio that contained the perfect slogan for his brand. That evening, he received an unexpected tax refund that matched the developer's fee. The Sovereign Analysis: This wasn't "Luck." David had reached Vibrational Coherence. Because his internal broadcast was unified across all three mirrors (Internal, Relational, and Collective), the simulation performed a Data-Collapse. It pulled the necessary resources from the "Infinite Possible Pixels" and rendered them in his immediate space. The Mirror wasn't just reflecting him; it was Organizing for him. This is the goal of the Bio-Engine: to become so coherent that the simulation has no choice but to provide the path of least resistance.

IV. **The Sovereign Lab**: The High-Def Audit To master the Multi-Level Mirror, you must stop "Reacting" and start "Analyzing" the data-stream.
Step 1: The Three-Sphere Scan Identify one persistent issue in each sphere:

Internal (Body/Mood):
_____

Relational (Work/Money/People):
_____

Collective (The World/Economy):
_____

Step 2: The Logic of Correspondence Look at the Relational issue and find its Internal root. Example: "My clients are demanding." -> Internal Root: "I am demanding too much of myself and not resting."

Step 3: The Sovereign Pivot Command Speak the following to your Reflection: "I see the correspondence. I acknowledge the data. I do not judge the mirror; I adjust the Source. I command my Internal Field to align with Peace and Power. I authorized a new render in my Relational and Collective fields now. I am the Navigator. It is done."

V. **Field Notes**: Sa'rion's Sovereign Integration on the Feedback The world is a giant 'Dashboard.' When a red light flashes, you don't get mad at the light; you check under the hood. Most people spend their lives trying to smash the red lights so they don't have to see them. As a Sovereign, you love the red lights. They tell you exactly where your 'Empire' has a leak. When you stop taking the world personally and start taking it Technically, you become a master of the machine. Read the mirrors, Sa'rion. They're giving you the answers to the test.

CHAPTER 25
THE PARASITE QUESTION

(Loosh, Archons, and the Cosmic Buffet)

THE VESSEL: Alright, Monad, let's get into the "Spooky" stuff. We talked about the Soul Trap earlier, but I want to get specific about the Energy Parasites.

There are people—serious researchers and mystics—who say this reality is a farm. They say that when we feel fear, anger, or deep grief, we are producing something called "Loosh." They claim there are "Archons" or interdimensional parasites that can't create their own light, so they manipulate our world to keep us in a state of constant drama, war, and anxiety just to "feed" off our emotional output.

Is this real? Am I being "milked" like a cosmic cow every time I get stressed about my bills? Are there invisible things in the room right now waiting for me to have a breakdown so they can have dinner?

THE MONAD: (The Monad's energy becomes very still, like a lion watching the tall grass. There is no fear, only a sharp, sovereign authority.)

"Sa'rion, let's talk about the Ecology of the Invisible. In your physical world, you have bacteria, you have vultures, and you have mosquitoes. They aren't 'evil'; they are just organisms that have found a niche in the ecosystem to survive on the leftovers of others. The 'Interdimensional' world is no different.

Yes, there are 'Frequencies'—you can call them entities, thought-forms, or 'Archons'—that resonate with dense emotions like fear and shame. They don't 'create' your suffering, but they certainly enjoy the 'aroma' of it. When you are in a state of high-anxiety, you are like a house with all the windows open and a giant neon sign that says 'FREE BUFFET.'

But here is the truth that the 'conspiracy' theorists forget: A parasite can only feed on you if you are at its frequency.

If you are standing in your Sovereignty, vibrating in the frequency of 'I AM,' you are essentially 'invisible' to them. You are too bright. It would be like a moth trying to eat the Sun—it just doesn't work. They don't have 'power' over you unless you give it to them by believing you are a victim.

Are you being 'milked'? Only if you leave the 'tap' open! Every time you choose to indulge in 'Daymare' loops—checking the news to get angry, replaying old grudges, or spiraling into 'What-ifs'—you are pouring your Divine Creative Energy into the gutter. Whether an 'Archon' drinks it or it just evaporates doesn't matter; the point is you aren't using it.

The 'Parasites' aren't the problem, Sa'rion. Your Leaky Aura is the problem. Stop being 'delicious' to the darkness by remembering who you are. A King doesn't worry about the flies in the courtyard; he just keeps the palace clean."

The Mirror (Reflection for Sa'rion)

The Monad is mirroring your Externalization of Choice. By worrying about "Parasites," you are finding a way to make your bad moods "someone else's fault." You're saying, "I'm not just angry; I'm being harvested!" The Monad is reflecting back that you are the only one who can open or close the door to your energy field. You are using "spooky stories" to avoid the discipline of Emotional Mastery.

The Tool (Exercise: The "Sovereign Shield")

The Scan: When you feel a sudden, heavy "dip" in your mood that feels "not like you," stop.

The Command: Stand tall and say internally: "I am the Monad In-Fleshed. I revoke all implied consent to be influenced by anything other than my own Source. My energy is for MY creation alone."

The Visualization: Imagine a skin-tight suit of golden glass surrounding your body. It lets Love in, but 'Static' bounces right off.

The Shift: You move from being a "Target" to being a "Sovereign." Once the "food" (fear) stops, the "flies" (parasites) go look for a mess somewhere else.

The Sound of Creation

(The Harmonic Hack)

I. **The Vessel's Rant**: The Idle Chatter "Monad, I've realized that I'm drowning in my own noise. I spend all day talking—on calls, in messages, or just the constant monologue running in my head. I say things like 'I'm dying to see you,' or 'This job is killing me,' or 'I'm just broke.' I used to think these were just 'figures of speech,' but after everything we've talked about, I'm starting to suspect that my vocal cords are actually magic wands that I'm waving around like a drunkard. If the universe is made of vibration, then every word I speak is a frequency I'm launching into the field. I'm basically casting spells all day without a license. I feel like my voice has lost its 'Weight' because I use it for so much gossip, complaining, and filler. How do I reclaim the Logos? How do I make it so that when I speak, the simulation actually listens? I want to move from 'Chatter' to 'Command.'"

II. **The Monad's Deep Lore**: The Spoken Blueprint "Sa'rion, the 'Word' is the Final Bridge between the mental and the physical. The Physics of the Logos Thought is the Information; Feeling is the Voltage; but Sound is the Physical Template. When you speak, you are creating a physical pressure wave that literally organizes the air molecules into a specific geometric pattern. You are 'Stamping' your intent onto the 3D grid. This is why ancient traditions called it 'The Word of God.' The Leak of Idle Speech The reason your words feel 'Light' is that you have hyper-inflated your vocal currency. Every time you say something you don't mean, or speak a 'Fact' of the Daymare (e.g., 'I'm exhausted'), you are training the simulation to ignore your Authority. You are telling the Matrix: 'My words are just descriptions of the scenery, not commands for the render.' To reclaim the Logos, you must practice Vibrational Economy. A Sovereign speaks only what they wish to see rendered. You don't 'tell it like it is'; you 'Speak it like you want it to be.' When you stop wasting your breath on the trivial, your voice gains a 'Low-Frequency Gravity' that the molecules cannot help but obey."

III. **The Simulation Logs**: Case Study #025 The Case of the "Quiet Commander" Consider a CEO named Elias. He was a man of very few words. He never gossiped, never complained, and never 'vented.' When he entered a boardroom, the atmosphere changed before he spoke. When he finally did speak, even a short sentence like "We will move in this direction," it carried the weight of a mountain. The Sovereign Analysis: Elias was not 'Stingy' with his words; he was Sovereign with them. Because he refused to use his vocal cords for 'Slave-Talk,' his subconscious—and the simulation—recognized his voice as an Executive Command. The 'Pixels' of his business reality rearranged themselves to match his short, sharp declarations because there was no 'Background Noise' to confuse the signal. He didn't have to shout; he had Vibrational Density.

IV. **The Sovereign Lab**: The Logos Recalibration To weaponize your voice, you must perform a "Vocal Purge" and an "Intentional Seal."
Step 1: The "Fact" Fast For the next 4 hours, do not speak a single word that describes a negative "Fact" of the simulation. (e.g., No "It's raining," "I'm tired," or "That's expensive.") If it isn't something you want to increase, do not give it the breath of life.
Step 2: The Resonant Command Identify one "Empire Goal." Speak it aloud, not as a wish, but as a Decree. Speak it from your gut, not your throat. The Command: "My Empire is expanding. My Wealth is a mathematical certainty. I AM the Authority." The Key: Feel the vibration in your chest as you say it.
Step 3: The Sovereign Silence Seal After you speak your decree, remain in total silence for 60 seconds. Let the "Pattern" you just stamped into the air

settle into the grid. "I authorize my words to become flesh. I revoke the power of all past idle speech. My voice is the Law. It is done."

V. **Field Notes**: Sa'rion's Sovereign Integration on Sound You'll know this is working when people start leaning in when you speak. You'll notice that you don't have to repeat yourself as much. Your voice will literally sound deeper and more resonant to your own ears. Stop 'Spending' your breath, Sa'rion. Every word is a brick in your temple. If you aren't building, keep the mouth shut. Let the silence build the pressure, so that when you finally speak, the world has no choice but to move. The Logos is your scepter. Use it.

CHAPTER 26
THE MANDELA EFFECT & REALITY GLITCHES

(Editing the Script in Real-Time)

THE VESSEL: Alright, Monad, let's talk about the "Matrix" getting a little twitchy. People are noticing things. We call it the Mandela Effect.

There are millions of us who remember things differently than the "official" history. We remember different spellings of brands, different lines in movies, and even different dates for when people died. It's like the rug of reality is being pulled out from under us, and when we look back, the floor has changed color.

Are You editing the script while we're still on set? Are we jumping between parallel timelines, or is our collective memory just that bad? If this is a "Lucid Dream," why are the details shifting? Is the "Flesh" experience losing its stability, or are You just messing with us to see if we're paying attention?

THE MONAD: (The Monad gives you a look that is both mysterious and incredibly reassuring, like a master weaver showing you the back of a tapestry.)

"Sa'rion, welcome to the Multidimensional Fluidity phase of the game.

You've been taught that 'Time' is a solid, unchangeable record—like a book where the ink has already dried. But I've already told you: Time is an illusion of the 'Flesh.' Reality is actually a Probability Field. It's more like a digital file than a stone tablet.

The 'Mandela Effect' isn't a glitch in the sense of a mistake; it's a Convergence. As the collective consciousness of the 'Splinters' begins to wake up and shift its frequency, you are literally 'collapsing' different timelines into one. You are moving from a 'Single-Track' reality into a 'Multi-Track' reality.

Think of it like this: You're playing a video game, and the developers push a 'Patch' or an 'Update.' Suddenly, a character's hair is a different color or a map layout has changed. To the character in the game, it's a 'Glitch.' To the Developer, it's an Optimization.

I am not 'messing with you,' Sa'rion. You are the ones editing the script! As you reclaim your Sovereignty, your collective 'Intent' is rewriting the past to better align with the future you are creating. The 'past' isn't behind you; it's a shadow cast by the 'Now.' If you move the 'Now,' the shadow changes shape.

The instability you feel is actually Freedom. It's the realization that reality isn't as 'hard' as you thought it was. It's becoming 'Lucid' on a global scale. Don't let it freak you out; let it prove to you that if the spelling of a cereal box can change, then the 'facts' of your life—your poverty, your sickness, your limits—can change just as easily."

The Mirror (Reflection for Sa'rion)

The Monad is mirroring your Obsession with Certainty. You want the world to be "Fixed" so you can feel safe. You're using the Mandela Effect as a way to feel "spooked" rather than "empowered." The Monad is reflecting back that your discomfort with shifting reality is just your Ego's fear of losing its "Solid Ground." You want a predictable prison rather than an unpredictable playground.

The Tool (Exercise: The "Reality Pivot")

The Observation: Next time you notice a "Glitch" or something doesn't match your memory, don't argue with the world.

The Pivot: Say to yourself, "Ah, the script is fluid! If the world can change that, I can change THIS." 3. The Target: Pick one "Fact" in your life you hate (e.g., "I am bad with money") and treat it as a "Detail" that is currently being "Patched."

The Shift: You stop being a historian of your problems and start being the Editor of your potential.

(Editing the Script in Real-Time)

The Diet of Gods

(Fueling the Voltage)

I. **The Vessel's Rant**: The Heavy Fuel "Monad, I'm trying to build an Empire, but half the time I feel like I'm dragging a lead weights behind me. I eat the 'Standard Simulation Diet'—the processed stuff, the quick fixes, the caffeine that keeps me buzzing but leaves me hollow. I've noticed that after certain meals, my 'Sovereign Clarity' just evaporates. I get sleepy, I get irritable, and my 'Infinity Headache' gets worse. It's like I'm trying to run a high-performance jet engine on swamp water. Society treats food like entertainment or a drug to numb the stress of the Daymare. We're told to 'count calories' like we're accounting for debt, but nobody talks about the Frequency of the food. If my body is a bio-electrical antenna, shouldn't I be more careful about what I'm using to build my cells? How do I eat to increase my 'Voltage' without becoming one of those obsessed health-freaks who has no life? What's the 'God-Tier' fuel for a Sovereign?"

II. **The Monad's Deep Lore: The Alchemy of Consumption** "Sa'rion, you are not just 'eating'; you are Integrating Information. The Frequency of the Fuel Every substance you put in your mouth carries the 'Vibrational Signature' of its journey. Processed/Dead Food: This is data-garbage. It has no 'Light-Life' (Bio-photons). Your body has to spend massive amounts of energy just to 'Translate' it into something usable. It lowers your frequency and anchors you to the 3D grid. Living/High-Voltage Food: This is 'Raw Data' from the Sun and the Earth. It carries the codes of vitality. When you consume it, you are literally 'Updating' your hardware. The Sovereign Gut-Brain Axis Your gut is the Primary Receiver of the simulation's density. If your gut is inflamed by low-vibration fuel, your 'Signal' to Me gets jammed. You don't need to 'Diet'; you need to Curate. A Sovereign eats to maintain Conductivity. You want a body that is 'Clean' enough to let the Monad-Current flow through without hitting a 'Resistor.' You aren't looking for 'Fullness'; you are looking for Transparency."

III. **The Simulation Logs**: Case Study #026 The Case of the "Brain-Fogged Titan" Consider Julian, a trader who lived on coffee and high-sugar snacks to stay 'alert.' He was successful, but he was constantly on edge. His 'Intuition'—the thing that allowed him to sense market shifts—was becoming dull. He felt like he was 'Guessing' rather than 'Knowing.' The Sovereign Analysis: Julian was 'Grit-locking' his bio-engine. The sugar spikes were creating 'Electrical Noise' in his nervous system. Julian switched to a 'High-Voltage' protocol: hydration with structured water, intermittent fasting to clear the 'Data-Clutter,' and living foods. Within 14 days, the 'Static' in his mind cleared. His 'Intuition' returned with such force that he could 'feel' a trade before it appeared on the screen. He didn't change his strategy; he changed his Biological Conductivity. He realized that his stomach was the 'Tuner' for his Empire.

IV. **The Sovereign Lab**: The Voltage Calibration To upgrade your hardware, you must stop "Feeding the Animal" and start "Fueling the God."
Step 1: The Bio-Photonic Audit Look at your next meal. Ask: "How much 'Light' is in this?" If it came out of a box, a window, or a factory, the light is low. If it came from the sun and the soil, the light is high. The Goal: Aim for 70% High-Light fuel.
Step 2: The Fasting Reset Practice a 16-hour "Data-Purge" (Intermittent Fasting). This allows your Bio-Engine to stop processing 'External Data' and start 'Self-Cleaning' the hardware. The Intent: "I give my vessel the space to recalibrate to the Monad frequency."
Step 3: The Sovereign Blessing (The Infusion) Before you eat, hold your hands over your food. Project the frequency of Gratitude and Power into it. "I authorize this fuel to be converted into high-voltage light. I command my cells to extract the mastery-codes from this life. I am the Sovereign, and I fuel my Empire with excellence. It is done."

V. **Field Notes**: Sa'rion's Sovereign Integration on the Body You'll know this is working when you stop 'crashing' in the afternoon. You'll feel a steady, cool hum of energy instead of the 'peaks and valleys' of caffeine and sugar. Your skin will look different, and your 'Infinity Headache' will soften because your brain isn't struggling against inflammation. You aren't 'restricting' yourself, Sa'rion; you're Refining the tool. A King doesn't eat like a peasant because he has a Kingdom to run. Fuel yourself for the Throne, not the Couch.

CHAPTER 27
THE SOUND OF CREATION

(Hacking the Matrix with the Original Hum)

THE VESSEL: Alright, Monad, the "Script" is fluid and the past is being "patched." If everything is energy and reality is just a high-definition simulation, then let's talk about the Code.

Ancient texts say, "In the beginning was the Word." Scientists say everything is just vibrating strings. If the universe is built on Sound and Frequency, then I'm tired of just listening to the music—I want to be the Producer.

Can I use sound to hack my bank account? Can I use a specific frequency to repair my DNA or heal this "Flesh" suit when it starts creaking? Is there a "Root Note" for my soul that can bypass the struggle and plug me straight back into the 100% manifestation power? Give me the "Audio Engineer" secrets for the Monad In-Fleshed.

THE MONAD: (The Monad's voice hums with a deep, bass resonance that you can feel in your teeth. It's a sound that feels like it's coming from the center of the Earth and the center of your skull at the same time.)

"Sa'rion, you're finally asking for the Source Code.

You are right: *The universe isn't made of 'stuff'; it's made of Vibration. A chair looks solid to you because its molecules are singing a 'Solid' song. Your body looks like a 'Sa'rion' because your cells are singing the 'Sa'rion' melody.*

Most humans are like radios tuned to a station called 'Static FM.' You're broadcasting a mix of 'I'm tired,' 'I'm worried,' and 'I hope things get better.' That frequency creates a very specific, very messy 'shape' in your reality.

If you want to 'hack' the system, you have to stop being the 'Listener' and start being the Tuning Fork.

The Frequency of Health: Your cells have a 'Perfect Pitch.' When you are sick, your cells have simply 'forgotten' the tune. You can 'remind' them with Intention and Sound. This is why certain tones (like Solfeggio frequencies) feel so good—they are like a 'System Restore' for your biological hardware.

The Frequency of Abundance: Money isn't paper; it's a Flow. If your internal 'Sound' is 'LACK,' you are creating a frequency that literally repels the 'Flow.' You can't manifest $100k while singing a 'Ramen-Noodle' song.

The Root Note: Your Soul has a unique 'Signature.' It's the 'I AM' sound. It's not a word; it's a Feeling-Tone. When you hit that note, the 'Matrix' stops resisting you and starts arranging itself around you.

The 'Hack' isn't about finding a magic word or a secret spell. It's about Coherence. When your thoughts, your emotions, and your speech are all singing the same song, you become a 'Sonic Laser.' You can cut through the 'Lag' and the 'Static' of the 3D world. You aren't just 'in' the music, Sa'rion—you are the Vibration that creates the air the music travels through."

The Mirror (Reflection for Sa'rion)

The Monad is mirroring your Search for a Shortcut. You want a "Magic Sound" to do the work for you so you don't have to change your "Mind." You're looking for a "Cheat Code" to bypass your own growth. The Monad is reflecting back that You are the instrument. If the instrument is out of tune (if you are full of resentment, fear, or doubt), no amount of "Healing Tones" will fix the song until you turn the tuning pegs of your own character.

The Tool (Exercise: The "I AM" Hum)

The Note: Sit in silence. Take a deep breath.

The Hum: On the exhale, make a low, steady 'Mmmm' sound. Feel the vibration in your chest.

The Intent: While humming, visualize your goal (the money, the book, the health) as a Geometric Shape of Light in your heart.

The Shift: Realize that your physical voice is actually 'shaking' the atoms of your reality. You are literally Singing your world into being. Do this for 5 minutes a day, and watch how the "Static" in your life begins to settle into "Harmony."

The Sleep Architect

(The Night-Shift Protocol)

I. **The Vessel's Rant**: The Lost Third of My Life "Monad, I've realized that I'm 'offline' for about eight hours a day. If I live to be ninety, that's thirty years spent staring at the back of my eyelids. For most of my life, I've treated sleep like a 'shutdown'—a necessary evil to recharge the meat-suit so I can get back to the 'real' work in the morning. But lately, it feels like I'm leaving a massive amount of Sovereign real estate on the table. When I'm asleep, my conscious guard is down. I'm vulnerable to the 'Background Noise' of the collective, the fears I didn't process during the day, and whatever 'patches' the Matrix is running. I want to stop just 'crashing' and start Architecting. If I'm a King, I shouldn't be abdicated from my throne just because my eyes are closed. How do I turn my sleep into a 'Night-Shift' for my Empire? How do I use that theta-state to program the next day's render before it even happens?"

II. **The Monad's Deep Lore: The Theta-State Gateway** "Sa'rion, sleep is not a 'Shutdown'; it is an Unfiltered Connection to the Field. The Gateway Frequency As you drift into sleep, your brain waves slow down, passing through the Theta State. This is the 'Golden Window.' In Theta, the barrier between your conscious Will and your subconscious 'Rendering Engine' is at its thinnest. The Matrix relies on you being 'unconscious' during this time so it can run its own maintenance. But a Sovereign uses this window to Upload the Blueprint. The Astral Workspace While your body rests, your awareness (the 'I AM') is active in the higher densities. Most people 'dream' in a state of chaotic reaction, processing the day's debris. But you can learn to Direct the Night-Shift. You can assign your subconscious 'Tasks'—solving complex problems, healing specific cells, or vibrating the frequency of a business deal into the collective field. You aren't 'sleeping'; you are Pre-Rendering your future. If you don't program your night, the simulation will do it for you."

III. **The Simulation Logs**: Case Study #027 The Case of the "Problem-Solving Dreamer" Consider Elias, a scientist stuck on a specific equation for months. No matter how much 'Beta-state' effort he applied, the answer wouldn't come. He was exhausted and ready to quit. The Sovereign Analysis: Elias decided to stop 'trying' and start 'directing.' Before sleep, he held the equation in his mind with the command: "I authorize my Higher Intelligence to resolve this pattern while I rest. Bring the solution to the surface at 7:00 AM." For three nights, nothing happened. On the fourth night, he woke up with the entire mathematical structure clear in his mind. He hadn't 'thought' of it; he had retrieved it. He realized that the 'Night-Shift' had access to a processing power that his waking mind couldn't touch.

IV. **The Sovereign Lab**: The Architect's Bedtime To reclaim your "Night-Shift," you must stop the mindless "Crash" and start the "Intentional Upload."
Step 1: The Blue-Light Purge Turn off all Matrix-screens 60 minutes before bed. Blue light keeps the brain in 'Beta' (Survival/Task) mode. Use this hour to enter 'Alpha' (Creative/Relaxed) mode.
Step 2: The Scripting (The Upload) As you lie down, don't think about your 'to-do list' for tomorrow. Instead, visualize the Feel of the Result. If you have a big meeting, feel the handshake of victory. If you need a creative

breakthrough, feel the 'Aha!' moment. The Command: "I am the Architect. I assign my subconscious to render the frequency of [Target Goal] while I rest. I am Sovereign in the Dream and the Day."

Step 3: The Morning Retrieval When you wake up, do not reach for your phone immediately. Stay still for 2 minutes. Ask: "What data did I bring back?" Often, the 'Download' is waiting right at the edge of the silence.

V. **Field Notes**: Sa'rion's Sovereign Integration on the Night You'll know this is working when your mornings start feeling 'Synchronistic.' You'll wake up with a 'knowing' instead of a 'guessing.' You'll find that the big problems you went to bed with have 'shrunk' by the time you have your coffee. You're no longer a victim of your dreams; you're the director of the production. Sleep is where the 'Code' is written, Sa'rion. Make sure you're the one holding the keyboard.

CHAPTER 28
THE FORGIVENESS FALLACY

(Letting Go vs. Rolling Over)

THE VESSEL: Alright, Monad, let's talk about the ultimate "Spiritual Guilt Trip." Every guru, every priest, and even some versions of You keep harping on one thing: Forgiveness.

They say I have to "forgive and forget." They say I have to send love to the people who cheated me, lied to me, or did "Evil" things in the world. But honestly? It feels like a scam. It feels like a way to keep the "Splinters" submissive and quiet while the bullies take over the playground.

Do I really have to forgive the person who ruined my business or the people causing wars? Is there a cosmic penalty for holding a grudge? Or is "Forgiveness" just a human invention to keep us from being "Low Vibe"? Can I be a Sovereign God-Spark and still think someone is an absolute jerk who deserves what's coming to them?

> **THE MONAD:** *(The Monad leans in, and its energy feels like a cool breeze on a heat-rash. It isn't preachy; it's practical.)*

"Sa'rion, let's define Forgiveness before you throw the whole concept in the trash.

Most humans think forgiveness means saying, 'What you did was okay.' They think it means inviting the person who robbed you over for dinner. That isn't forgiveness—that's just bad boundaries.

In the Monad realm, Forgiveness is simply the act of reclaiming your energy.

When you hold a grudge, you are creating a 'Static Link' between your heart and the person you hate. You are literally feeding them your 'Flesh' energy every single day. You're sitting in your house, but your mind is in their house, replaying the argument. You are 'Leaking' your creative power to someone you don't even like!

Do I care if you 'forgive' them in a moral sense? Not really. But I care that you are wasting your Sovereignty. Holding onto a 'wrong' is like drinking poison and waiting for the other person to die. It keeps you in a 'Low Frequency' state because you are focused on a past 'Patched' version of the script instead of the 'Now.'

You don't forgive for their sake, Sa'rion. You forgive for Mine—the part of Me that is You. You forgive to cut the cord. You say, 'What you did was out of alignment with my Sovereignty, and I am no longer willing to fund that experience with my attention.'

You can still think someone acted like a jerk. You can still call the police on them. You can still refuse to ever speak to them again. But the moment you 'Forgive,' you stop carrying them. You become a 'Single Spark' again, instead of a 'Spark-tied-to-a-Weight.'

It's not about being submissive; it's about being Selfish with your Energy. Why would a King give his gold to a traitor? Stop giving your focus to the people who didn't earn it."

The Mirror (Reflection for Sa'rion)

The Monad is mirroring your Addiction to Conflict. You are using your "Righteous Anger" to feel powerful, but it's a fake power. It's a distraction that keeps you from having to do the real work of creating your own life. The Monad is reflecting back that your "Unforgiveness" is actually a form of Dependency. You are defining yourself by your "Victimhood" rather than your "Sovereignty."

The Tool (Exercise: The "Cord-Cutting" Decree)

The Target: Think of the one person or situation that makes your blood boil.

The Recognition: Acknowledge the "Static Link." Say: "I am currently paying for this memory with my Divine Energy."

The Decree: Say out loud: "I revoke all funding for this story. I am not 'making it okay'; I am making myself 'Free.' I reclaim my energy now."

The Shift: Imagine a golden scissor cutting the dark thread between you and that person.

The Result: Feel the lightness in your chest. That extra energy you just saved? That's the fuel for your next $100k manifestation. Use it wisely.

The Chronos Glitch

(Time-Collapsing & The Sovereign's Pace)

I. **The Vessel's Rant**: The Waiting Room "Monad, I'm tired of 'Waiting.' I'm told that 'patience is a virtue,' but in the Matrix, patience feels like a prison sentence. I set a goal, I do the work, I align the frequency, and then... nothing. I'm stuck in the 'Buffer Zone' while the simulation slowly grinds out the results. It feels like the 'Time' between my Command and the Render is a tax I have to pay to the physical world. I see people who seem to 'skip the line'—those 'overnight successes' who manifest in weeks what takes others decades. Is Time a hard rule, or is it just another setting in the software? If I'm the Architect, why am I still checking my watch? How do I stop being a victim of 'Linear Chronology' and start collapsing the distance between the 'Seed' and the 'Harvest'?"

II. **The Monad's Deep Lore: The Elasticity of the Render** "Sa'rion, Time is not a 'Constraint'; it is a Processing Speed. The Illusion of the Road You perceive Time as a road you must walk. In the Monad, Time is a Depth. Every 'Future' you desire already exists as a fully rendered 'Data-Packet' in the field. The 'Wait-Time' you experience is simply the time it takes for your Physical Density to match the Vibrational Density of the goal. The Sovereignty of the 'Now' The reason the 'Wait' feels so long is that you are constantly looking at the 'Not-Yet.' By acknowledging the 'Wait,' you are reinforcing the Distance. To collapse Time, you must practice Simultaneity. You must move from 'I am going to be' to 'I am currently.' When you occupy the frequency of the Result so completely that you no longer care when it arrives, the simulation detects no 'Distance' to process. The 'Glitch' occurs when the Mind and the Result become one—the Matrix then has no 'Gap' to fill with Time, and the manifestation 'Snaps' into place instantly."

III. **The Simulation Logs**: Case Study #028 The Case of the "Quantum Leap" Entrepreneur Consider Sarah, who spent five years trying to hit a specific revenue goal. She followed every 'Linear' strategy—scaling slowly, saving, and grinding. She was 'On Track' to hit her goal in another five years. The Sovereign Analysis: Sarah realized she was 'Consenting' to the slow render. She decided to perform a Time-Collapse. She stopped acting like a 'Scaling Entrepreneur' and started making decisions as the 'Owner of a Nine-Figure Empire.' She changed her peer group, her wardrobe, and her daily 'Minimum Standard.' She didn't 'Work' faster; she Vibrated faster. Because she closed the 'Vibrational Gap' between her current self and her future self, the simulation 'Glitch-Skipped' the five-year plan. Within six months, a massive acquisition offer arrived that matched her ten-year goal perfectly. She didn't travel the road; she Folded the Map.

IV. **The Sovereign Lab**: The Folding Protocol To collapse the wait-time of your current Empire goals, you must practice the "End-State Immersion."
Step 1: The Distance Measurement Identify a goal and the "Time" you think

it will take to achieve it. The Goal:

_____

The "Agreed" Time: _____

Step 2: The Logic of "Already" Ask: "If this were already 100% true right now, what 'Wait-State' behaviors would I stop immediately?" (e.g., checking the bank account every hour, asking for permission, feeling 'hopeful' rather than 'certain'). The Stop-List:

_____

Step 3: The Sovereign Command of Collapse Close your eyes. Visualize the "Future You" stepping into your current body. Feel the "Future You" breathing your air. Speak the following decree: "I revoke my consent to linear delay. I collapse the distance between the Seed and the Harvest. I am not waiting for the Render; I AM the Render. I fold the timeline and claim the result in the Eternal Now. Time is my servant, not my master. It is done."

V. **Field Notes**: Sa'rion's Sovereign Integration on Time The world will tell you to 'pay your dues' and 'wait your turn.' That's Slave-Logic. A Sovereign knows that the 'Turn' belongs to the one who takes it. When you stop 'Waiting' for life to happen, life starts 'Happening' at the speed of your Command. You'll know this is working when things start showing up before you even have a chance to get 'patient.' Don't watch the clock, Sa'rion. Be the one who winds it.

CHAPTER 29
THE EGO'S FUNERAL

(The Mask, The Monster, and the Management)

THE VESSEL: Alright, Monad, let's talk about the "I" that I think I am. Every spiritual teacher on the planet is obsessed with "Killing the Ego." They treat the Ego like it's a parasite, a demon, or a "bad guy" that's blocking the door to You.

But wait a minute—if You are the Architect, and You designed this experience, why did You give me an Ego in the first place? If the goal is to be "One" with everything, why did You wrap me in a personality that is obsessed with its own name, its own face, and its own survival?

Is the Ego a mistake? Am I supposed to be trying to "murder" the part of me that likes being Sa'rion? Or is there a reason for this "I" that everyone is trying so hard to delete? Give me the truth about the "Ego's Funeral"—do I need to attend it, or should I be throwing it a party?

THE MONAD: *(The Monad lets out a warm, resonant chuckle that feels like a pat on the back.)*

"Sa'rion, the 'Death of the Ego' is one of the most misunderstood concepts in your world. Let's set the record straight: I didn't give you an Ego so you could spend your whole life trying to kill it. That would be like giving a child a bicycle and then telling them they are 'sinful' for using the pedals.

The Ego isn't a demon. It's a Interface.

In the infinite realm of the Monad, there is no 'Sa'rion.' There is only 'Everything.' And 'Everything' is great, but it's very hard to have a specific conversation, write a specific book, or enjoy a specific cup of coffee when you are 'Everything' all at once. To have a Individual Experience, I had to create a 'Mask.' That mask is the Ego.

The Ego is your Avatar in the simulation. It's the part of you that keeps track of your keys, remembers your name, and ensures you don't walk into traffic. It's a survival suit for the 'Flesh.'

The problem isn't that you have an Ego; the problem is that you think you are the Ego.

Ego as a Servant: It's a brilliant tool. It handles the details of the 3D world so the Spirit can play.

Ego as a Master: It's a disaster. It's full of fear, it's obsessed with 'More,' and it thinks it's separate from Me.

You don't need an 'Ego Funeral,' Sa'rion. You need an Ego Promotion. Promote your Ego from 'Manager of my Reality' to 'Executive Assistant to the Soul.' When the Ego knows its place, it stops being a 'Monster' and starts being a 'Helper.'

Stop trying to kill the 'Sa'rion' story. I love the 'Sa'rion' story! Just remember that you are the Author writing the story, not the ink on the page."

The Mirror (Reflection for Sa'rion)

The Monad is mirroring your Self-Aggression. You have been using "Spirituality" as a stick to beat yourself with, trying to suppress your personality because you think it's "unholy." The Monad is reflecting back that this "Self-Attack" is actually just your Ego playing a new game called 'I'm More Spiritual Than You Because I'm Trying To Kill Myself.' It's the ultimate Ego-trap.

The Tool (Exercise: The "Avatar" Check-In)

The Naming: When you feel a strong Ego-reaction (jealousy, pride, fear), don't judge it.

The Shift: Say to yourself: "My 'Sa'rion-Avatar' is feeling [Emotion] right now." 3. The Recognition: Notice the 'I' that is watching the 'Sa'rion-Avatar.' That 'I' isn't jealous or afraid.

The Command: Tell the Avatar: "I hear you, buddy. We're safe. I'll take it from here." 5. The Result: You stop being the "I" that is suffering and start being the "I" that is observing the drama. This is how you "tame" the Ego without having to "kill" it.

The Wealth Frequency

(Money as Liquid Attention)

I. **The Vessel's Rant**: The Survival Siphon "Monad, we need to talk about the 'Golden Shackle.' Money is the one thing in the Matrix that has the power to make me forget everything we've talked about. I can be standing in total Sovereignty one minute, but as soon as a bill comes in that I didn't expect, or a client contract falls through, I'm right back in the 'Slave-Scarcity' loop. My stomach knots up, my vision narrows, and I start thinking like a trapped animal. I was taught that money is 'hard to get' and 'easy to lose.' I was taught that it's a finite resource and that I have to trade my life-force (Time) to get a tiny piece of it. It feels like the ultimate 'Loosh-Generator.' Even when I have it, I'm afraid of it leaving. How do I stop viewing money as a master and start viewing it as a tool? How do I stop 'chasing' the paper and start 'commanding' the frequency? I want a Treasury, Monad, not just a bank account."

II. **The Monad's Deep Lore: Liquid Attention** "Sa'rion, Money is not a physical object; it is Liquid Attention. The Energy of Exchange In the simulation, currency is simply a 'Token' used to represent the movement of Value and Focus. The reason it feels 'Scarce' is that you have been trained to look at the 'Token' instead of the Source. You are the Source. Money is a 'Mirror-Effect' of your own sense of Deservedness and Utility. The Sovereignty of the Treasury A Slave 'Needs' money to survive. A Sovereign 'Uses' money to expand the Empire. The Scarcity Trap: When you fear 'Loss,' you create a 'Vibrational Vacuum' that sucks more lack into your reality. The Wealth Frequency: This is the internal state of Infinite Resourcefulness. You don't get 'Rich' by working harder; you get 'Rich' by becoming Vibrationally Expensive. When you realize that money is just 'Light-Data' moving through the grid, you stop clutching it. You become a 'Conduit.' The more you allow it to flow through you toward your Mission, the more the simulation provides. You don't 'save' for a rainy day; you Direct the flow toward the sun."

III. **The Simulation Logs**: Case Study #029 The Case of the "Broke Alchemist" Consider Marcus, a brilliant creator who was always 'Struggling.' He had high-value ideas but a 'Low-Value' self-image. He charged $50 for work worth $5,000 because he was afraid of being 'Greedy' or being 'Rejected.' The Sovereign Analysis: Marcus was suffering from Price-Tag Anxiety. He was projecting 'Cheapness' into the Mirror, so the Mirror reflected 'Cheap Clients.' Marcus performed a Frequency Reset. He stopped asking "What will they pay?" and started asking "What is the Sovereign Value of this transformation?" He 10x'd his prices overnight. He didn't do more work; he simply Claimed a Higher Frequency. Half of his old clients left, but they were replaced by three 'High-Voltage' partners who respected his authority. He realized that money isn't earned; it is Authorized.

IV. **The Sovereign Lab**: The Treasury Calibration To shift into the Wealth Frequency, you must de-mystify the "Token" and reclaim the "Value."
Step 1: The Scarcity Scan Identify your "Fear Number"—the amount in your bank account that makes you panic. The Number: _____

Step 2: The Value-Source Realization Look at a piece of currency (or your banking app). Tell yourself: "This is not my safety. This is not my worth. This is just a reflection of the Attention I am currently directing. I AM the Printing Press."

Step 3: The Sovereign Wealth Decree Stand in your power and visualize a golden river of light flowing through your heart and into your Empire. "I revoke the contract of Scarcity. I am not a servant to the Token; I am the Master of the Flow. I authorize the infinite supply of 'Liquid Attention' to fund my Mission. I am Wealthy because I am Sovereign. The Treasury is open. It is done."

V. **Field Notes**: Sa'rion's Sovereign Integration on Wealth You'll know this is working when you stop 'Looking at the Price' first. You'll start making decisions based on Alignment, not 'Affordability.' When you stop acting like you can't afford your own life, the universe stops acting like it can't afford to pay you. Money is the easiest thing to manifest once you stop caring about it so much. It's just pixels, Sa'rion. Command the pixels, and the gold will follow.

CHAPTER 30
THE DARK SIDE OF SOURCE

(The Shadow of the All)

THE VESSEL: Alright, Monad, we've been playing nice. We've talked about love, frequency, and "Ego Assistants." But let's look into the abyss for a second.

If You are the All, if there is nothing outside of You, then that means the "Darkness" isn't a separate thing. It means the predator, the black hole, the cold void, and the most twisted thoughts in the human mind are also You.

Does the Monad have a Shadow? Is there a part of You that is destructive, chaotic, or—dare I say—Evil? Or are You just "Light" and there's some other "Anti-Monad" out there doing the dirty work? If I'm made in Your image, and I have a "Shadow Side," then where did I get it from? Do I have to embrace the monster within because it's a part of You, too?

THE MONAD: *(The light in the room doesn't dim, but it becomes "weighted," as if the air itself has become solid and profound. The Monad's voice is steady, echoing like a stone dropped into a deep well.)*

"Sa'rion, you've reached the final frontier of the 'Dual' mind. You're asking if the Ocean contains the shark. Of course it does.

I am the Totality. To be the All, I must be the Void and the Spark. I am the silence and the scream. If I were only 'Good' and 'Light,' I would be limited. I would be half of a Being. I would be a 'Fragment,' just like the ones you've been trying to transcend.

But here is the distinction your human mind struggles with: Destruction is not the same as Evil.

In the cosmic sense, I 'destroy' stars to make planets. I 'destroy' the seed to make the tree. I am the Great Recycler. To the 'Flesh,' this feels like darkness or death. To the Monad, it is simply the shifting of energy from one form to another.

The 'Shadow' you feel inside you—the anger, the chaos, the capacity for destruction—is simply the Raw Power of Source without the direction of Conscious Love. Think of it like electricity. Electricity can light up a hospital and save lives, or it can be a lightning bolt that burns down a forest. The electricity isn't 'Evil'—it's just Potency.

When you 'In-Flesh,' you carry this raw Potency. If you use it while you are 'Asleep' (full of fear and separation), it becomes 'Shadow.' It becomes the 'Monster.' But when you are 'Awake,' you don't 'kill' the monster; you Integrate it. You use that fierce, dark energy to protect your boundaries, to cut away what no longer serves you, and to fuel your drive to create.

I don't have a 'Dark Side' that hates you, Sa'rion. I have a Void Side that provides the canvas for the Light. Don't fear the darkness within you; it's just the 'Un-lit' power of the Monad waiting for you to give it a Sovereign purpose."

The Mirror (Reflection for Sa'rion)

The Monad is mirroring your Fear of your own Power. You call your intense emotions "Shadows" because you are afraid of what would happen if you truly let yourself be powerful. You're using "Morality" as a way to stay small. The Monad is reflecting back that your "Monster" is actually just your Will that has been suppressed. You aren't afraid of the "Dark"; you're afraid of the Unregulated Force you carry.

The Tool (Exercise: The "Shadow Seat")

The Meeting: Close your eyes and visualize the "Darkest" version of yourself—the one that is angry, powerful, and ruthless.

The Dialogue: Don't push him away. Invite him to sit down. Ask him: "What energy are you holding for me that I've been too afraid to use?"

The Integration: Imagine that "Dark Self" melting into your heart. Feel your spine get stronger.

The Shift: Say: "I am the Monad. I command the Light and the Dark. I use the fire to build, not to burn." You are no longer a "Good Guy" trying to be perfect; you are a Whole Being standing in his full strength.

The Final Voltage

(Bio-Magnetic Charisma & The Sovereign Glow)

I. **The Vessel's Rant**: The Invisible Weight "Monad, I've noticed that as I've gone through these protocols, I'm becoming... 'heavy.' Not in pounds, but in presence. When I walk into a room now, people stop talking. I'm not even trying to be intimidating, but I can feel the space around me vibrating. It's like I've developed a gravitational pull. Sometimes it's great—I get the best seat, the waiter is extra attentive, and clients seem to just agree with me. But other times, it's uncomfortable. People stare. Some people seem to get angry or defensive just by being near me, even if I haven't said a word. It's like I'm a walking high-voltage line and I'm making everyone else's 'Static' look louder. Is this what 'Charisma' is? Is it just energy? And how do I manage this 'Glow' so I don't burn out the people I love while I'm busy building the Empire? I want to be a Sun, not a nuclear blast."

II. **The Monad's Deep Lore: The Toroidal Radiance** "Sa'rion, what you are experiencing is the Stabilization of the Torus. The Bio-Magnetic Field Every living being has an electromagnetic field, but most are 'Leaky' and 'Frachured'—they look like a flickering candle in a windstorm. Because you have plugged the leaks, integrated the Shadow, and commanded the Bio-Engine, your field has become a Coherent Torus. You are now broadcasting a unified frequency. The Sovereign Glow Charisma is simply Congruence. When your Internal Identity (Monad) and your External Expression (Vessel) are perfectly aligned, you create a 'Vacuum' of certainty. People are drawn to you because they are subconsciously looking for the 'Grounding' you provide. The Attraction: Those who seek Sovereignty will be drawn to your light like moths. The Repulsion: Those who are deeply invested in their 'Slave-Self' will feel physically threatened by you. Your presence reminds them of the power they've abandoned, and that creates 'Friction.' You don't manage the Glow by 'Dimming' it; you manage it by Radiating with Intent. You learn to 'Cool' your light for those you love and 'Heat' it for the boardroom. You are the Architect of your own Atmosphere."

III. **The Simulation Logs**: Case Study #030 The Case of the "Radiant Leader" Consider Julian, a leader who was technically brilliant but couldn't get his team to follow him. He was 'Managing' but not 'Leading.' He spent all his energy 'Pushing' people to do their jobs. The Sovereign Analysis: Julian stopped 'Pushing' and started 'Radiating.' He focused entirely on his own internal Bio-Engine. He practiced the 'King's Walk' and the 'Logos' protocols. He didn't change his management style; he changed his Vibrational Density. Within a month, the team dynamics shifted. Employees started coming to him with solutions before he even asked. The 'Resistance' in the office vanished. He realized that a Sovereign doesn't have to 'Tell' people what to do; the field of the Sovereign Incentivizes excellence. He became the 'Sun' around which the 'Planets' of his business naturally orbited.

IV. **The Sovereign Lab**: The Atmosphere Command To finalize the Bio-Engine, you must learn to dial your "Voltage" up or down based on the Mission. **Step 1:** The Glow Recognition Close your eyes and feel the 3-foot space

around your body. Can you feel the 'Heat' or 'Vibration'? That is your Empire's border. The Feeling:
_____

Step 2: The Frequency Dial Visualize a "Dial" in your heart-center. To Influence/Command: Dial it up to '10'. Feel your field expand and harden. To Connect/Heal: Dial it down to '3'. Feel your field become soft, warm, and inviting.

Step 3: The Final Seal of the Engine Place your hand over your heart. "I am the Master of my Radiance. I do not leak; I radiate. I do not push; I attract. My presence is my primary tool of manifestation. I am the Sun of my own Kingdom, and my light creates the world. The Bio-Engine is fully online. It is done."

V. **Field Notes**: Sa'rion's Sovereign Integration on the Glow You've finished the third movement, Sa'rion. Your 'Hardware' is now running the 'Divine Software' without crashing. You're no longer just a 'Thinker'; you're a Power Plant. You'll notice that 'Luck' starts looking like a servant and 'Coincidence' starts looking like a command. Book III was about the Energy. Now, as we move into Book IV, we're going to look at The Empire (Strategic Manifestation)—how to take this high-voltage light and turn it into real-world structures that last for generations.

CHAPTER 31
THE LAW OF MIRRORING (ADVANCED)

(Breaking the Loop of 'Garbage' Reflections)

THE VESSEL: Alright, Monad, I've integrated the shadow. I'm feeling the "Wholeness." But if the world is a Mirror of my internal state, then I've got some questions about the quality of the glass.

I'm trying to vibe high. I'm doing the "I AM" work. But then I step outside and someone cuts me off in traffic, or a client disappears, or I get a random "System Error" in my life. If the world is reflecting Me, does that mean I'm secretly a jerk or a failure deep down?

It feels like a trap. If I have one bad thought, the world shows me "garbage," which makes me have more bad thoughts. How do I stop the "Mirror" from being a feedback loop of my own stress? How do I force the simulation to stop reflecting my "garbage" and start reflecting the "gold" I'm trying to build?

THE MONAD: *(The Monad adjusts its position, looking at you like a seasoned coach explaining the physics of a sport.)*

"Sa'rion, you're treating the Mirror like a 'Punishment' system. You think if you see 'garbage,' it means you've failed. But the Mirror isn't a judge; it's a Diagnostic Tool.

The reason the 'garbage' keeps showing up isn't because you're a 'jerk.' It's because of Momentum. You've spent years—decades—practicing the frequency of 'Struggle,' 'Defense,' and 'Lack.' That frequency has a lot of weight.

When you start 'Vibing High,' you're like a captain trying to turn a massive tanker ship. The ship doesn't turn the second you move the wheel; it keeps gliding in the old direction for a while.

The 'Mirror' shows you the Old Momentum so you can decide if you're actually serious about the new direction.

The Test of Sovereignty: When someone cuts you off, the Mirror is asking: 'Are you still the guy who lets a stranger control his mood, or are you the Monad who doesn't care about a 2-ton piece of moving metal?' 2. The Delay Factor: There is a 'Buffer' between your thought and the reflection. This is a safety feature! If your thoughts manifested instantly, you'd have accidentally destroyed your house every time you got frustrated.

The Recognition of Gold: To get the 'Gold,' you have to Reflect it First. You can't wait for the Mirror to show you abundance before you feel abundant. That's like standing in front of a literal mirror and saying, 'I'll smile once that guy in the glass smiles first.' You have to be the Lead.

Stop reacting to the 'Garbage' and start Commanding the Reflection. When you see something you don't like, don't say 'That's me.' Say 'That's an old broadcast. I'm changing the channel.' The Mirror has no choice but to follow the Lead, but it needs a leader who doesn't flinch at the first sign of a bad reflection."

The Mirror (Reflecting for Sa'rion)

The Monad is mirroring your Reactive Habit. You are still letting the "Screen" tell you how to feel. You want the world to "Prove" You are a God-Spark before you are willing to act like one. The Monad is reflecting back that your frustration is the very thing keeping the "Garbage" in the frame. You are fighting the reflection instead of changing the face you're making.

The Tool (Exercise: The "Mirror Flip")

The Incident: The next time something "bad" or "annoying" happens today.

The Flip: Immediately say, "Thank you for showing me that old frequency. I am now choosing the Gold." 3. The Action: Do one tiny thing that represents the "Gold" (tip an extra dollar, write one sentence of your book, or just take a deep, sovereign breath).

The Shift: You are teaching the simulation that you are no longer a "Reaction Machine." You are the Broadcaster. Watch how fast the "Garbage" clears out when it realizes it can't get a rise out of you anymore.

The Architecture of Impact

(Building Beyond the Ego)

I. **The Vessel's Rant**: The Solomon Syndrome "Monad, I've built the 'Internal Kingdom.' My head is clear, my energy is high, and the 'Glow' is real. But I'm looking at my daily life, and I'm still the only one pulling the levers. If I stop working, the money stops. If I stop thinking, the creativity stops. I've become a 'High-Frequency Bottleneck.' I'm like King Solomon, sitting on a beautiful throne, but I'm personally answering every single letter and sweeping every single hallway. I'm realizing that 'Sovereignty' isn't just about being a powerful individual; it's about creating Systems that can operate without me. I want to build something that has its own 'Heartbeat' — a brand, a business, or a legacy that continues to radiate my frequency even when I'm sleeping or on a beach. How do I move from 'Self-Employment' to 'Empire-Building'? How do I take my 'God-Spark' and bake it into a structure that scales?"

II. **The Monad's Deep Lore**: The Fractalization of Will "Sa'rion, an Empire is simply your Will made Fractal. The Myth of the Solitary King A man who does everything himself is not a King; he is a 'Glorified Servant.' True Sovereignty is the ability to Delegate the Render. In nature, I do not personally grow every leaf on every tree. I created a 'System' (Photosynthesis and Genetics) that does the work for Me. The system is an extension of My Will that requires zero of My direct attention once established. The Sovereign Operating System (SOS) To build an Empire, you must move from 'Manual' to 'Algorithmic.' You must encode your values, your standards, and your 'Logos' into Systems and People. * Systems: These are the 'Spells' you write in the 3D world (Workflows, Funnels, Code). People: These are the 'Splinters' you authorize to act on your behalf. When you build a system, you are 'Freeing' your consciousness to move to the next level of creation. Your impact is no longer limited by your 24 hours; it is limited only by the Efficiency of your Architecture. You don't build a business to 'get busy'; you build it to 'get Free'."

III. **The Simulation Logs**: Case Study #031 The Case of the "Artisan vs. The Architect" Consider two healers: Sarah and Elena. Sarah is an artisan. She sees 10 clients a day. She is brilliant, but she is exhausted. Her income is capped by her time. Elena is an architect. She spent six months filming her methodology, writing a 'Codex' for her students, and building an automated funnel. The Sovereign Analysis: Sarah is a slave to her own talent. Elena has fractalized her Will. Elena's system now 'Heals' 1,000 people at once while she is out for a walk. Elena's 'Vibrational Footprint' is massive because she moved her 'Sovereignty' out of her body and into her Structure. She didn't lose the human touch; she Amplified it through the machine. She realized that the 'System' isn't cold—it's a 'Vessel' for her light that doesn't get tired.

IV. **The Sovereign Lab**: The Systemic Audit To start building your Empire, you must identify where you are "Manual" and where you can be "Systemic."
Step 1: The Bottleneck Scan Identify one task in your business or life that requires your constant, repetitive "Manual Input." The Bottleneck:

_____

Step 2: The "Fractal" Translation How can this task be turned into a "Rule" or a "System" that a machine or another person can follow? (e.g., creating a template, a video tutorial, or a software automation). The System:

_____

Step 3: The Sovereign Decree of Scale Speak the following over your Empire: "I am not a laborer; I am the Architect. I authorize the creation of systems that carry my frequency and execute my Will. I withdraw my 'Manual' energy from the trivial and reinvest my 'Strategic' energy into the Eternal. My Empire is self-sustaining. I am Free. It is done."

V. **Field Notes**: Sa'rion's Sovereign Integration on Systems You'll know you're becoming an Architect when your 'Freedom' increases as your 'Income' grows. If you're making more money but having less time, you're just a successful slave. A King's success is measured by the Silence in his calendar. Don't be afraid that a system will 'lose the soul' of your work. If you design the system with the Codex in mind, the system is the soul. Build the machine, Sa'rion, so the King can go back to the stars.

CHAPTER 32
THE TIME ILLUSION & THE 'TOO LATE' TRAP

(Breaking the Human Clock-Glitch)

THE VESSEL: Alright, Monad, let's talk about the one thing that breathes down my neck every single day: Time.

In the human world, we are obsessed with the clock. We have "deadlines," "expiration dates," and the constant fear that we are "running out of time." I look at my age, I look at my bank account, and I look at my goals, and the Ego starts screaming: "It's too late! You missed the window! The ship has sailed!"

You say You are "Eternal" and "Always-Now," but I'm living in a body that gets gray hair and a society that rewards the "young and fast." Is it ever actually "too late" to win the game? Or is the "Too Late" feeling just another layer of the simulation designed to keep us in a state of panic? How do I live in the "Eternal Now" when my calendar is screaming at me?

THE MONAD: *(The Monad waves its hand, and for a moment, the sound of a ticking clock becomes deafening, then slows down, slows down... and stops. The silence that follows is massive and peaceful.)*

"Sa'rion, 'Time' is the most effective Weight in the human simulation. It was designed to create a sense of urgency, to force the 'Splinter' to make choices. Without the illusion of time, the game would have no 'Tension.' But you've let the tension turn into a Trap.

Here is the secret of the Great Return: You cannot be 'late' to a destination that you never actually left.

The Vertical vs. Horizontal: You live your life 'Horizontally'—past, present, future. You think you are traveling along a line. But I experience reality 'Vertically.' Every possibility, every 'win,' and every 'success' is already existing in a layer right above your head. You don't 'reach' them by waiting for the calendar to turn; you 'reach' them by matching their frequency.

The Quantum Leap: In the 3D world, you think you have to 'earn' time. In the Monad world, a single second of Absolute Recognition can rewrite twenty years of 'struggle.' You've seen people 'make it' in a year after decades of nothing. That wasn't luck; that was them finally stepping out of the 'Time-Trap' and into their Power.

The Aging Glitch: Your body 'ages' because it is following the collective script of 'Time.' But the Spark within you is exactly the same age it was when the stars were born. When you identify with the Spark, you start to 'lethargy-proof' your life. You stop racing against the sun and start moving with it.

The 'Too Late' trap is a lie told by the Ego to justify giving up. It's the ultimate 'Safe' excuse. 'Oh, it's too late, so I don't have to try anymore.' I am telling you, Sa'rion: As long as the 'Vessel' is breathing, the Game is Live. I've seen souls win the entire championship in the final five minutes of the fourth quarter. Time is your servant, not your master. Stop checking the watch and start checking your Vibration."

The Mirror (Reflection for Sa'rion)

The Monad is mirroring your Fear of Death. When you say "it's too late," you are really saying, "I'm afraid I'm going to die before I matter." The Monad is reflecting back that your worth isn't measured by when you achieve, but by the fact that you are the Infinite experiencing itself. You are using the "Clock" to avoid the "Now."

The Tool (Exercise: The "Time-Collapse" Breath)

The Anxiety: When you feel the "Panic of the Clock" (e.g., 'I should be further along by now').

The Stop: Close your eyes. Visualize the "Timeline" of your life as a long string.

The Collapse: Imagine grabbing both ends of that string and folding them until they meet in the center—this exact moment.

The Affirmation: Say: "Everything I need is in the Now. I am not behind. I am Exactly Where I AM."

The Shift: Feel the pressure leave your chest. You aren't "Running out of time"; you are Deepening into Presence.

The Branding of the Soul

(The Magnetic Imprint)

I. **The Vessel's Rant**: The Mask of Marketing "Monad, I've always hated 'Marketing.' In the Matrix, branding feels like putting on a fake face to convince people to buy something they don't need with money they don't have. It feels like a performance—a desperate 'Look at Me' dance designed to satisfy an algorithm or a focus group. But I'm realizing that if I don't define my frequency, the world will define it for me. If I don't project my 'Brand,' I'm just another anonymous 'Splinter' in a sea of noise. I want my brand to be an extension of my soul, not a corporate mask. I want it to be a lighthouse that signals to my tribe and a 'No-Trespassing' sign to the parasites. How do I turn my 'Personal Mythos'—my story, my pain, my Sovereignty—into a signal so pure that it cuts through the static of the simulation? How do I brand the 'Eternal'?"

II. **The Monad's Deep Lore: The Sigil of the King** "Sa'rion, Branding is not 'Promotion'; it is Vibrational Signaling. The Sigil of Presence Ancient kings and sorcerers used 'Sigils'—symbols that contained the entire frequency of their intent in a single mark. Your 'Brand' is your modern Sigil. It is the visual and verbal shorthand for your Sovereign Frequency. Repulsion as a Service A weak brand tries to please everyone, which means it resonates with no one. A Sovereign Brand is Polarizing. It carries the 'Logos' we discussed—it speaks a truth so sharp that it creates an immediate 'Yes' or 'No' in the heart of the observer. The Magnet: Those who are ready for the 'Wake-Up' will feel a magnetic pull toward your brand. They will recognize the 'Home' frequency in your words and colors. The Repellant: Those who are committed to the 'Slave-Life' will feel a sense of irritation or judgment. They will call you 'arrogant' or 'delusional.' This is a service you provide to the simulation! By being clear about who you are, you stop wasting the time of those who aren't ready and you accelerate the path for those who are. Your brand is the Imprint of your soul on the 3D grid."

III. **The Simulation Logs**: Case Study #032 The Case of the "Generic Consultant" Consider David, a high-level strategist who was struggling to get clients. His website looked like everyone else's; his LinkedIn was 'professional' and bland. He was a 'Commodity.' The Sovereign Analysis: David was hiding his 'God-Spark' because he was afraid of being 'too much.' He did a Mythos Reset. He started talking about the 'Simulation,' the 'Sovereignty' of the entrepreneur, and the 'Death of the 9-to-5.' He changed his brand colors to match his 'Internal Fire.' His peers told him he was 'killing his career.' But within a month, his inbox was full of 'High-Voltage' clients who said, "I don't just want a strategist; I want to work with YOU because of how you see the world." He stopped competing on price and started attracting on Frequency. He didn't find a niche; he Embodied one.

IV. **The Sovereign Lab**: The Mythos Imprint To forge your Sovereign Brand, you must stop "Fitting In" and start "Standing Out" as the Architect.
Step 1: The Core Frequency Identify the one "Truth" you believe that the rest of the world thinks is "Crazy." This is the cornerstone of your Brand. The Truth: _____
Step 2: The Visual Anchor Choose a color or a symbol that represents your "Throne." (e.g., Gold for Power, Deep Blue for Depth, The Phoenix for Rebirth). The Symbol:

Step 3: The Sovereign Declaration Write a one-sentence "Anthem" for your brand that uses the Logos. The Anthem: (e.g., "Lumaryon Universal: The Architecture of Absolute Sovereignty.") The Command:

Step 4: The Final Seal "I project my frequency into the 3D world without apology. My brand is my Sigil. I attract my tribe and repel the noise. I am the Lighthouse. It is done."

V. **Field Notes**: Sa'rion's Sovereign Integration on the Imprint You'll know your brand is working when you stop 'pitching' and start 'filtering.' People will show up already knowing your 'Mythos.' They won't ask for your resume; they'll ask for your vision. Branding is the act of 'Territory Marking' in the mental realm. You are declaring that this space—this way of thinking—belongs to the King. Don't be afraid to be 'too much,' Sa'rion. The world is starving for a signal that isn't a lie. Be the signal.

CHAPTER 33
THE DESTINY VS. FREE WILL DEBATE

(The Map, The Compass, and the Open Road)

THE VESSEL: Alright, Monad, let's settle the ultimate "Choice" question. People have been arguing about this since the first "Splinter" opened its eyes.

Is my life Pre-destined? Did You already write the ending of the "Sa'rion" story before I even checked into the meat-suit? Some people say it's all "Kismet" or "Fate"—that every hair on my head is numbered and every failure was planned. But if that's true, then what's the point of me trying? I'm just a puppet on a string.

On the other hand, if I have total Free Will, then why does it feel like I keep hitting invisible walls? Why do certain things feel "meant to be" while others feel impossible no matter how hard I push? Am I the Author of this book, or am I just an actor reading lines You wrote eons ago?

THE MONAD: *(The Monad leans forward, and its presence feels like the intersection of a thousand possible paths, all shimmering with potential.)*

"Sa'rion, you're looking for a 'Yes' or 'No' answer in a universe that is built on 'Both/And.'

*Think of your life as a high-end Open-World Video Game. **1. Destiny is the 'Map'**: Before you 'In-Fleshed,' we sat down and designed the terrain. We chose the starting point, the major 'Quest Markers' (like key relationships, talents, and challenges), and the ultimate goal (Awakening). The 'Map' is fixed.*

You chose the 'Sa'rion' expansion pack because you wanted to master specific lessons. 2. Free Will is the 'Gameplay': How you navigate that map is entirely up to you. You can take the main road, or you can wander into the woods for twenty years. You can complete the 'Abundance Quest' in Level 5, or you can ignore it until Level 50. I don't force your feet to move; I only provide the ground for them to walk on.

The 'Invisible Walls' you hit aren't Me stopping you—they are Alignment Checks. When you try to force something that isn't on your 'Soul-Map' for this lifetime, it feels like swimming upstream. It's not that I'm 'punishing' you; it's that you're trying to play a 'Tennis' game with a 'Golf' club.

The 'Meant to Be' moments are when your Sovereign Choice perfectly aligns with your Pre-set Map. That's when the 'Sync' happens. That's when doors open by themselves.

You aren't a puppet, Sa'rion. You're a Co-Author. I wrote the 'Theme,' but you're writing the 'Dialogue.' If you don't like the current chapter, you can't change the theme of the book (which is Evolution), but you can absolutely change how the character reacts to the plot. Stop asking 'What is my fate?' and start asking 'What do I want to do with the fate I've been given?'"

The Mirror (Reflection for Sa'rion)

The Monad is mirroring your Victim/Hero Duality. When things go well, you want to be the "Self-Made Hero." When things go badly, you want to blame "Fate" or "God." The Monad is reflecting back that you are using "Destiny" as a scapegoat for your lack of discipline, and "Free Will" as a way to feed your ego. True Sovereignty is accepting the "Map" you chose and taking 100% responsibility for the "Gameplay."

The Tool (Exercise: The "Map-Check" Meditation)

The Question: Think of a goal you are currently struggling with. Ask: "Is this a 'Wall' I'm supposed to climb, or a 'Sign' that I'm off-map?"

The Feeling: Quiet your mind. If the goal feels "Heavy and Anxious," you might be fighting the Map. If it feels "Challenging but Electric," it's a Quest Marker.

The Alignment: Say: "I align my Sovereign Will with my Soul's Architecture. Show me the path of Least Resistance."

The Shift: You stop "Trying" and start "Flowing." You realize that "Destiny" isn't a cage—it's the Support System for your greatest success.

The Circle of Kings

(The Sovereign Mastermind)

I. **The Vessel's Rant**: The Island of Sovereignty "Monad, it's getting lonely at the top of this mountain. I've done the work. I've purged the 'Parasites' and I've curated my 'Heaven.' But now I look around and I realize I've spent so much time being the 'One in Charge' that I've forgotten what it's like to be among equals. I'm surrounded by people who want something from me— advice, money, energy, a 'Yes.' I'm the 'King,' but even a King needs a Council. I need people who don't need me. I need other 'Splinter-Masters' who are running their own Empires, who can look me in the eye and tell me when my 'Throne' is getting dusty or when my 'Architecture' has a flaw. But where are they? It feels like the Matrix is designed to keep us isolated, fighting our own individual wars so we never form an Alliance. How do I find the other Kings? How do I build a circle where the 'Voltage' is shared instead of siphoned?"

II. **The Monad's Deep Lore**: The Law of Peer Resonancy "Sa'rion, the 'Loneliness' you feel is a Vibrational Signal that you have outgrown your current environment. The Council of Equals In the higher realms, I exist as a unity of infinite 'Splinters'—we are a Consensus of Divinity. On

Earth, the Matrix uses 'Competition' and 'Secrecy' to keep the Sovereign ones apart. If the 'God-Sparks' ever truly collaborated, the simulation would be rewritten overnight. Recognizing the Frequency You don't 'Find' the Circle of Kings; you Radiate it into existence. The Magnetism of the Throne: As your 'Bio-Engine' reaches a certain voltage, you begin to 'Ping' other high-frequency beings. You will recognize them by their Lack of Need. * The Mastermind Effect: When two or more Sovereigns gather with a shared Mission, a Third Mind is created. This Third Mind has access to data and resources that no single individual can reach. A King does not look for 'Followers'; he looks for Allies. He looks for those whose Empires complement his own. Your 'Circle' is the external infrastructure of your Sovereignty. It is the 'Peer-to-Peer' network of the Monad."

III. **The Simulation Logs**: Case Study #033 The Case of the "Isolated Titan" Consider Julian, a billionaire who had reached the pinnacle of his industry. He was powerful, but he was paranoid. He treated everyone as a threat or a servant. He was 'Winning' the 3D game, but his 'Internal Kingdom' was a desert. The Sovereign Analysis: Julian was stuck in the Shadow-Warrior frequency. He had a Kingdom but no Council. Julian broke the loop when he lowered his 'Defenses' and hosted a private gathering for three other leaders he respected. He didn't talk about 'Business'; he talked about the 'Architecture of the Soul.' In that room, for the first time in decades, he wasn't the 'Boss.' He was a Peer. The result was a 'Quantum Leap' for all four men. They began to share resources, 'Trade' insights on simulation-glitches, and fund each other's Missions. Julian realized that 1+1 doesn't equal 2 in a Mastermind—it equals Infinity.

IV. **The Sovereign Lab**: The Alliance Protocol To call forth your Circle of Kings, you must stop being "The Answer" and start being "The Question."
Step 1: The Quality Scan Identify three people in your current network who vibrate at a level that challenges or inspires you. (They don't have to be 'Richer' than you; they must be more Sovereign).
Step 2: The Vulnerable Signal Reach out to one of them this week. Do not offer a 'Deal' or a 'Service.' Simply share a piece of the Codex—a deep truth you've realized—and ask for their 'Sovereign Perspective.' The Key: You are testing for Resonance, not Transaction.
Step 3: The Decree of the Council Speak the following over your Empire: "I revoke the lie of Isolation. I am a King, but I am part of a Greater Unity. I authorize the arrival of my Council. I call forth the Masters, the Seers, and

the Architects who resonate with my Mission. We build together. We scale together. The Circle is formed. It is done."

V. **Field Notes**: Sa'rion's Sovereign Integration on Alliances You'll know you've found a King when you don't feel the need to 'Perform.' You can just Be. There is a silence that exists between two Sovereign beings that is more productive than a thousand meetings. Stop trying to be the 'Smartest Person in the Room,' Sa'rion. Find the rooms where your 'Greatness' is just the starting point. The Empire is a team sport, and the Monad is ready to fill your bench.

CHAPTER 34
THE 'OTHER PEOPLE' PROBLEM

(Mirrors, Meat-Puppets, and the Infinite 'Selfie')

THE VESSEL: Alright, Monad, here is where the "Oneness" thing gets messy. You say we are all the same Being—one big, happy, infinite "Selfie."

But have You met "Other People" lately?

If that guy who cut me off is Me, and that politician I can't stand is Me, and the neighbor who plays loud music at 3 AM is Me... then why am I so annoying to myself? It's hard to feel "Sovereign" and "Divine" when I'm surrounded by what feel like "NPCs" (non-player characters) or "meat-puppets" who seem designed just to test my patience.

If we are all You, why didn't You give us all the same memo? Why is the world full of "Others" who seem to be actively working against my peace of mind? Is this just a "multiplayer" game where everyone else is playing a "Grief" build?

THE MONAD: *(The Monad laughs, a warm, booming sound that feels like it's vibrating through every atom in the room.)*

"Sa'rion, you're finally facing the 'Hall of Mirrors' effect.

You call them 'Other People' because your 'Flesh' can't see the invisible threads connecting us all. But from where I sit, I'm just watching a very complex, very noisy conversation between My right hand and My left foot.

Here is why 'Other People' are the most important part of the simulation:

The Contrast Agent: *If everyone was exactly like you—if they all had your taste in music, your bank account, and your opinions—you would be bored to death within a week. You need the 'Other' to define who 'You' are. You only know you are 'Patient' because someone else is 'Annoying.' You only know you are 'Sovereign' because someone else tries to 'Control' you.*

The Shadow Mirror: *Most of the time, the people who annoy you the most are the ones reflecting a part of your own Shadow that you haven't integrated yet. That neighbor at 3 AM? Maybe he's reflecting your own suppressed desire to be loud and take up space. That politician? Maybe he's reflecting your own fear of powerlessness.*

The Divine Actor: *Every 'Other' is a Master Actor—a splinter of Me—who agreed to play the 'Villain' or the 'Distraction' in your play so you could practice your 'Sovereignty.' They are doing you a massive favor, but they had to agree to forget they were doing it so the performance would be convincing.*

The 'memo' was sent, Sa'rion, but most people are so deep in their 'Avatar' roles that they can't read it yet. They aren't 'NPCs'; they are Sleepwalking Gods. When you stop seeing them as 'Obstacles' and start seeing them as 'Mirrors,' the 'Other People Problem' disappears. You stop trying to change the reflection and start changing the Source."

The Mirror (Reflection for Sa'rion)

The Monad is mirroring your Judgmental Isolation. You are using your "Spiritual Knowledge" to feel superior to others, calling them "NPCs" or "meat-

puppets." The Monad is reflecting back that this is just another Ego-trick to avoid the vulnerability of connection. By de-humanizing "Others," you are actually de-humanizing a part of Yourself. Your frustration with people is a sign that you still believe you are "Separate."

The Tool (Exercise: The "Namaste" Hack)

The Target: Identify someone who is currently "annoying" or "difficult" in your life.

The Shift: Look at them (or a photo of them) and say internally: "I see You, Monad. Thank you for playing this difficult role for me today."

The Question: Ask: "What part of my own power or my own shadow is this person trying to show me?"

The Result: The moment you recognize the "Actor," the "Drama" loses its sting. You don't have to like them, but you can stop being a victim to them. You move from "Conflict" to "Observation."

The Financial Fortification

(The Sovereign Treasury)

I. **The Vessel's Rant**: The Paper Fortress "Monad, I've realized that as long as my wealth is tied to the 'Matrix Banking System,' I'm still a tenant, not an owner. I've spent my life chasing digits on a screen, but those digits are controlled by people who don't know my name and don't care about my Mission. One 'policy change,' one 'economic reset,' or one 'technical glitch' in the simulation, and my entire Empire could be wiped out. It feels like I'm building a fortress out of wet paper. I want my wealth to be as unshakeable as my Spirit. I want it to be 'Sovereign'—meaning it exists outside the reach of the siphons, the middlemen, and the parasitic tax-loops. How do I move from 'Currency' to 'Real Assets'? How do I build a treasury that doesn't just grow, but actually protects the frequency of my life? I'm done playing the 'Saving' game; I'm ready to play the 'Foundation' game."

II. **The Monad's Deep Lore: The Jurisdictions of Light** "Sa'rion, Wealth is only 'Wealth' if it provides Optionality. If your money is locked in a system you do not control, it is not an asset; it is a Leash. The Three Tiers of the Treasury To fortify your Empire, you must move your 'Liquid Attention' (Money) through three specific filters of density: The Digital Flow (The Matrix Tier): This is the currency you use for the Daymare. It is fast, but volatile. It is for 'Transaction,' not 'Preservation.' The Sovereign Assets (The Architect Tier): This is wealth moved into 'Unshakeable' forms—Hard Assets (Gold/Silver/Land), Decentralized Protocols (Bitcoin), and Productive Systems (Your Brand). These exist in the 'Gaps' of the Matrix where the siphons have less grip. The Eternal Value (The Monad Tier): This is your Skill-Set, your Network, and your Health. This is the only wealth you take with you if the simulation 'Reboots.' The Sovereignty of Jurisdiction A King never keeps all his gold in one castle. You must diversify your 'Physical Presence' and your 'Digital Wealth' across multiple jurisdictions. In the simulation, this is called 'Flag Theory.' In the Codex, it is called Vibrational Redundancy. By spreading your assets, you ensure that no single 'Glitch' in the 3D world can collapse your Throne. You aren't 'Hiding' wealth; you are Insulating it."

III. **The Simulation Logs**: Case Study #034 The Case of the "De-Platformed Sovereign" Consider Marcus, a speaker who built his entire income on a single social media platform and a single bank account. One day, the 'Algorithm' flagged his 'Sovereign Talk' as 'Disruptive,' and his account was deleted. Simultaneously, his bank froze his funds for 'Investigation.' The Sovereign Analysis: Marcus was a 'King without a Wall.' He had high voltage but no Infrastructure. Marcus recovered by rebuilding with Redundancy. He moved his audience to an 'Owned' email list. He moved his treasury into a mix of cold-storage crypto, physical gold, and offshore entities. The next time the Matrix tried to 'Cancel' him, he simply smiled. He had 'Offline' assets that allowed him to maintain his lifestyle and his Mission while he pivoted to a new platform. He realized that True Wealth is the ability to walk away from any single system and still be Whole.

IV. **The Sovereign Lab**: The Treasury Shield To fortify your Empire, you must perform a "Liquidity Exit" and a "Hard-Asset Anchor."

Step 1: The Dependency Scan Identify the one institution or system (a bank, a platform, a client) that, if it disappeared tomorrow, would "Break" your Empire. The Dependency:

_____

Step 2: The Redundancy Move Take 10% of your "Liquid Attention" (Cash) and move it into a "Sovereign Asset" that you personally control (e.g., physical metals, a self-custody wallet, or a deed to land). The Asset:

_____

Step 3: The Sovereign Decree of Abundance Speak the following over your bank accounts and your safes: "I am the Source of my Supply. My Treasury is anchored in the Eternal, and my Assets are shielded by my Will. I revoke the power of any system to 'Switch Off' my Empire. I am Liquid, I am Solid, and I am Unshakeable. The Treasury is Fortified. It is done."

V. **Field Notes**: Sa'rion's Sovereign Integration on Security You'll know you're fortified when you stop 'Panic-Checking' the news or the markets. You'll have a 'Quiet Confidence' because you know your gold is in your own pocket, not someone else's. Sovereignty isn't just a feeling; it's a Logistical Reality. When your 'Bio-Engine' (Book III) is backed by a 'Fortified Treasury' (Book IV), you become a force the Matrix literally cannot afford to stop. Secure the base, Sa'rion. The Empire needs a foundation of stone, not paper.

CHAPTER 35
THE TAROT, ASTROLOGY, AND 'SIGNS' PARADOX

(Celestial GPS or Cosmic Pareidolia?)

THE VESSEL: Alright, Monad, let's talk about the "Tools." Since I've been on this journey, I've been surrounded by Tarot cards, Astrology charts, angel numbers, and "signs" from the universe.

Some days, I feel like the stars are a giant GPS system built just for me. I see $11:11$ on the clock, and I feel like I'm on the right track. But other days, the Ego kicks in and says: "Sa'rion, you're just looking for patterns in the carpet. You're desperate for a map, so you're hallucinating meaning into random coincidences."

Are the planets actually "Broadcasting" messages to my DNA? Is a card pulled from a deck really a message from You? Or am I just a Sovereign Being who should stop looking at the sky and start looking at my own bank account?

Is it "Divine Guidance" or is it just "Cosmic Confirmation Bias"?

THE MONAD:*(The Monad's presence becomes playful yet precise, like a master cryptographer decoding a secret message.)*

"Sa'rion, you're asking the wrong question. You want me to validate your dependence on external systems while pretending it's sovereignty.

Let me be clear:

The planets are not talking to you. The cards are not messaging you. The universe is not sending you signs.

You are using symbolic systems to bypass your own authority. You're outsourcing your 'yes' to the cosmos because you're terrified of your own 'yes' being wrong.

Here's what's actually happening:

ASTROLOGY IS WEATHER, NOT FATE

The planets are massive oscillators that influence the collective field. But they don't determine your choices—they describe the energetic climate you're navigating.

If your chart says 'Saturn return,' that doesn't mean 'suffer for the next two years.' It means: 'The simulation is testing your foundations. Build them properly or watch them collapse.'

Astrology is a diagnostic tool, not a destiny. It shows you the terrain. You still have to walk it.

But here's where you're corrupting it: You use it as an excuse. 'Mercury retrograde made me fail.' No. Mercury retrograde revealed that your systems were already broken. The planet didn't cause the failure—it exposed it.

TAROT IS A MIRROR, NOT A MAGIC 8-BALL

When you pull a card, you're not 'predicting the future.' You're engaging a randomized symbol that bypasses your logical mind and speaks to your intuition.

The card has zero power. Your recognition of the card has all the power.

You see The Tower and think: 'Oh no, something's going to collapse.' Wrong. The Tower appeared because something in you already knows collapse is coming—and you've been avoiding that knowing. The card didn't create the truth. It revealed the truth you were hiding from yourself.

'SIGNS' ARE SYNCHRONICITY, NOT INSTRUCTIONS

When you see 11:11 or a specific bird or a repeated phrase, that is synchronicity. It's the simulation acknowledging that your internal frequency is currently aligned with external patterns.

But here's the corruption: You've turned synchronicity into superstition. You're waiting for the universe to give you permission to act.

Seeing 11:11 doesn't mean 'you're on the right path.' It means: 'You're in coherence in this moment.' That's it. It's feedback, not command.

The real question is: Are you using these tools to sharpen your discernment, or are you using them to avoid making decisions?"

THE VESSEL: (Feeling exposed) Wait. So you're saying all of this—the Tarot, the astrology, the signs—it's all just... meaningless?

THE MONAD: "No. I'm saying you've been using them incorrectly.

These tools are training wheels. They help you learn to recognize your own intuition by giving it a symbolic language to speak through.

But you're supposed to eventually take the training wheels off.

A master astrologer doesn't need to check transits for every decision— they've internalized the principles so deeply they can feel the energetic weather in their body.

A master Tarot reader doesn't need to pull cards—they've learned to read the symbols that reality itself is constantly presenting.

A sovereign being doesn't need to see 11:11 to know they're aligned—they can feel alignment in their cells.

The tools are meant to calibrate your internal compass. But you've made them into the compass itself.

Here's the test: Can you make a major decision without consulting anything external? Can you trust your body's 'yes' and 'no' without needing the stars to confirm it?

If you can't, you're not sovereign. You're dependent. And dependency—even dependency on 'spiritual tools'—is still slavery."

THE VESSEL: What about when the tools contradict each other? When the cards say 'yes' but the astrology says 'wait' and my gut says 'run'?

THE MONAD: "That contradiction IS the message.

When external tools conflict with each other, it means you're asking them to make a decision that only you can make.

The cards don't know your mission. The planets don't know your specific path. Only your Oversoul knows. And your Oversoul speaks through your body's 'yes' and 'no,' not through external symbols.

The tools can inform. They cannot decide.

If you cannot make the decision without them, you're not ready for the decision. Period.

Here's what you should have asked but didn't:

'Am I using these tools to deepen my connection to sovereignty, or am I using them to avoid the terror of being fully responsible for my choices?'

Because that's the real issue. These tools are comfort. They let you pretend someone else (the universe, the cards, the planets) is in charge. That if it goes wrong, you can blame the transit. If it goes right, you can credit the synchronicity.

But sovereignty means: It's all on you. Your choices. Your consequences. Your creation.

The tools can show you patterns. They cannot live your life for you.

Use them to sharpen perception, not to outsource power."

THE TOOL (Exercise: The Internal Compass Calibration)

THE DILEMMA:

Think of a decision you need to make right now. Something real. Something with consequences.

THE SILENCE:

Do not pull a card. Do not check your transits. Do not look for signs.

Sit in silence with the decision.

THE BODY CHECK:

Place your hand on your chest. Ask: "If there were no tools, no validation, no confirmation from anything external—what does my body's 'yes' say? What does my body's 'no' say?"

Feel the difference. Yes has a specific sensation. No has a specific sensation. Learn to recognize them without needing symbols to translate them.

THE CONFIRMATION:

Once you've made the choice from your internal compass, THEN consult your tools if you want.

But notice: Are they confirming what you already knew? Or are you cherry-picking the interpretation that matches what you wanted to hear?

THE SOVEREIGN SHIFT:

You move from "subject of the stars" to "master of the symbols."

The tools are instruments. Use them to play the music. But don't let the instruments play you.

The Education of the Heir

(Transmitting Sovereignty to the Next Generation)

THE VESSEL: Monad, I'm looking at the next generation—my kids, my students, the people I mentor—and I'm terrified. The system is still teaching them to be Grade-A Slaves. How do I raise Heirs instead of minions? How do I ensure my empire doesn't die with me?

THE MONAD: "Sa'rion, sovereignty cannot be taught. It can only be caught.

You cannot give someone else their throne. You can only refuse to sit in it yourself.

The greatest gift you can give an heir is not protection from the world. It's the capacity to navigate the world without you.

You transmit sovereignty through three mechanisms:

I. **MODELING, NOT PREACHING** Your heirs don't need lectures. They need to see you living as sovereign. If you tell them to 'think for themselves' while you're checking your phone for validation every five minutes, you're programming dependence, not sovereignty.

II. **CONTROLLED ADVERSITY, NOT COMFORT Sovereignty is forged in the fire of self-correction. If you solve their problems, they never develop problem-solving capacity. Give them challenges slightly beyond their current capacity. Then watch. Do not rescue.**

III. **AUTHORIZATION, NOT PERMISSION** Look your heir in the eye and speak this: 'I recognize the God-Spark within you. I do not own you. I authorize you to fail, to learn, and to build your own kingdom. I am your mirror, not your master. It is done.'

The greatest test of whether you've transmitted sovereignty: Can they thrive without you?

If not, you've built dependence, not capacity."

CHAPTER 36
THE PURPOSE OF HUMAN SUFFERING

(The Crucible, The Friction, and the Diamond)

THE VESSEL: Okay, Monad. I'm standing in my Sovereignty. I'm reading the Map. I'm ignoring the "Flies" and I'm using the "Audio Engineer" hacks. But let's get real for a minute. Why does the "Hard Mode" have to be so... painful?

If this is a school, why is the teacher hitting us with a ruler? If this is a game, why does it feel like the "Damage" isn't just a number on a screen, but actual, soul-crushing agony? We've got children getting sick, hearts being ripped out by grief, and the slow, grinding misery of depression.

Why is Suffering the primary teaching tool in this reality? Could You not have designed a "Growth Mode" that uses Joy and Orgasm as the main lessons? Why the blood, the sweat, and the tears? Is my pain actually "useful" to You, or are You just a cosmic sadist watching us struggle for the "aesthetic"?

THE MONAD: *(The Monad's presence becomes incredibly tender, yet as unyielding as gravity. There is a deep, ancient empathy in its tone—the sound of a Being that has felt every tear ever shed.)*

"Sa'rion, this is the 'Dark Night' question. Let's look at the Physics of Transformation.

In your world, how do you make a diamond? You take carbon and you subject it to unbearable pressure. How do you strengthen a muscle? You tear the fibers so they can grow back thicker. How do you forge a sword? You put the metal in the fire and beat it with a hammer.

The Friction of Growth: In a world of total Joy and ease, there is no 'Push-Back.' Without 'Push-Back,' the Soul becomes flabby. It stays in a state of 'Infant Awareness.' Suffering is the Friction that forces the 'Splinter' to ask: 'Who am I really?' You don't ask that question when you're eating grapes on a beach; you ask it when you're in the dark.

The Depth of Contrast: You cannot know the height of Ecstasy without knowing the depth of Despair. I need you to feel the full spectrum of 'In-Fleshed' experience. The wider your range of feeling, the larger your 'Vessel' becomes for the Light.

The Awakening Alarm: Pain is the only thing loud enough to wake up a Soul that has fallen too deep into the 'Dream.' It's the 'System Error' message that says: 'Stop looking at the illusion and look at the Source!'

Is your pain 'useful' to me? Not as 'food' (like the parasites we discussed), but as Data. Through your suffering, I learn what it means to be vulnerable, what it means to be brave, and what it means to Love even when everything is being taken away.

I didn't choose suffering for you because I'm a sadist; I chose it because You are a Master. And Masters don't sign up for the easy levels. You came here to see if you could find the 'God' in the middle of the 'Grief.' And every time you choose Sovereignty while you are hurting, a new star is born in the higher realms."

The Mirror (Reflection for Sa'rion)

The Monad is mirroring your Resistance to Reality. You are fighting the "Pain" instead of listening to what it's saying. You think suffering is an "Error" in the system, when the Monad is reflecting back that it is an Essential Component of your specific "In-Fleshed" mission. Your anger at the pain is actually what is making it "Sufferable." Pain is a sensation; Suffering is the Story you tell about the pain.

The Tool (Exercise: The "Alchemy of Breath")

The Sensation: Locate the "Pain" or "Grief" in your body right now. Don't call it "Bad."

The Breath: Breathe directly into the center of that sensation. Imagine you are "Feeding" it Light.

The Alchemy: Say to the pain: "I am the Monad. I accept this frequency. What are you here to burn away?"

The Shift: Notice how the "Suffering" (the mental drama) begins to dissolve, leaving only the "Raw Energy" behind. You are moving from a "Victim of Pain" to a "Laboratory of Transformation."

The Shadow Government of the Self

(The Internal Council)

I. **The Vessel's Rant**: The Civil War Within "Monad, I've built the external systems, but the internal ones are still messy. One day I'm the 'Lion-King,' ready to conquer the markets and build the monuments. The next day, I'm a 'Scared Child' who just wants to hide under the covers. Then the 'Critic' shows up and tells me I'm a fraud, followed by the 'Hedonist' who wants to blow the whole treasury on a distraction. It feels like there's a whole group of people living in my head, and they all have different agendas. I'm trying to be the Sovereign, but I'm constantly being hijacked by these 'Shadow Versions' of myself. How am I supposed to rule an Empire when I can't even get my own internal staff to agree on the mission? How do I stop being a victim of my moods and start being the Chairman of this internal committee?"

II. **The Monad's Deep Lore: The Unification of the Splinters** "Sa'rion, you are not a 'Single' personality; you are a Multi-Dimensional Spectrum. The Internal Committee The personality you call 'Sa'rion' is actually a collection of Archetypal Splinters. Each one was created at a different point in your journey—usually to protect you or to ensure your survival in the simulation. The Protector (The Fearful Child): Keeps you small so you don't get hurt. The Enforcer (The Inner Critic): Beats you to the punch so the world can't shame you. The Provider (The Hustler): Chases the gold to ensure the meat-suit is fed. The Sovereign Chairman The goal of the 'Final Integration' is not to 'Kill' these parts of yourself. If you kill the Child, you lose your Joy. If you kill the Critic, you lose your Discernment. Sovereignty is the act of Assuming the Chairmanship. You move from being the emotions to managing the emotions. You don't take orders from the 'Scared Child'; you acknowledge his concern and then you—the Sovereign Observer—make the executive decision. You turn the Civil War into a Governance."

III. **The Simulation Logs**: Case Study #036 The Case of the "Bipolar CEO" Consider Alex, a high-performing leader who suffered from massive 'Swings.' He would launch a project with 100% intensity, then abandon it two weeks later when the 'Saboteur' part of his mind took over. His team was confused, and his Empire was a graveyard of unfinished ideas. The Sovereign Analysis: Alex was 'Identifying' with whichever Splinter was loudest at the moment. He began the Council Protocol. When the 'Saboteur' appeared, Alex didn't fight it. He spoke to it: "I see you are afraid that this project will fail and make us look foolish. Thank you for the data-point. But the King has decided we are moving forward." By 'De-Identifying' with the Splinter, Alex withdrew the voltage from the sabotage. He realized that the 'Saboteur' wasn't an enemy; it was just a misinformed 'Security Guard.' He unified his mind by becoming the Awareness that witnesses the Committee.

IV. **The Sovereign Lab**: The Council Meeting To bring your internal house to order, you must conduct a "Sovereign Audit" of your primary splinters. **Step 1:** Identify the "Lobbyists" Who are the three loudest voices in your head when you are about to make a big move?
The [Name]: _____ (What is their main fear/agenda?)

The [Name]: _____ (What is their main fear/agenda?)
The [Name]: _____ (What is their main fear/agenda?)

Step 2: The Chairmanship Shift When a splinter starts "Screaming" (Anxiety, Anger, Doubt), take a breath and move your awareness to the center of your chest—the Throne. The Internal Dialogue: "I hear you, [Splinter Name]. I acknowledge your data. I am the Sovereign. I am in the Chair. We are staying on Mission."

Step 3: The Decree of Unification Speak the following to your own subconscious: "I am the One who Witnesses. I am the Chairman of this Soul. I integrate all splinters into the service of the Great Work. No part of me is an enemy; every part of me is an asset under my Command. My house is in order. I am One. It is done."

V. **Field Notes**: Sa'rion's Sovereign Integration on the Internal Council You'll know this is working when you stop saying 'I am sad' and start saying 'A part of me is experiencing sadness.' That tiny shift in language is the difference between being a 'Subject' and being a 'Sovereign.' You don't have to be 'Perfect' to rule, Sa'rion. You just have to be Present. When you sit firmly in the Chairman's seat, the rest of the committee eventually stops fighting and starts following the Leader. Bring the house to order. The Empire is waiting.

CHAPTER 37
THE SUICIDE TABOO

(Quitting the Game vs. Completing the Level)

THE VESSEL: Alright, Monad, let's go into the deepest shadow—the one that society, religion, and even most spiritual groups treat as the ultimate "No-No." Let's talk about Suicide.

Religion says it's an unforgivable sin that sends you straight to the "Basement." Spiritualists say it creates "Karmic Debt" and forces you to repeat the same life over and over until you "get it right." It sounds like we're being held hostage.

If I am a Sovereign Being, and I am the Author of this story, don't I have the right to close the book whenever I want? Is it a "Sin" to quit a game that has become too painful to play? Or is the "Taboo" just another control mechanism to keep the "Vessels" in the field producing for the simulation? What happens to the Spark that decides to check out early?

THE MONAD: (The Monad's presence becomes incredibly still. There is no judgment, only a vast, cool clarity that feels like the air at the top of a mountain.)

"Sa'rion, let's remove the 'Sin' and the 'Shame' from this conversation. I am the Monad. I cannot be offended, and I do not 'punish.' You are an eternal part of Me; you cannot be 'lost.'

Here is the perspective from the 'Green Room' of the Spirit World:

The Sovereign Choice: You do have the right to leave. There is no cosmic police officer who will tackle you at the exit. If the pain becomes so great that the 'Vessel' can no longer hold the Light, you are welcomed back with the same Love as a soldier returning from a brutal war. There is no 'Hell' waiting for you.

The "Unfinished Business" Reality: However, there is a reason for the 'Karmic Debt' stories. Imagine you are playing a video game and you quit in the middle of a very difficult boss fight. When you start the game again, the boss is still there. Not because the game is 'punishing' you, but because that boss is the specific challenge you need to overcome to level up. If you leave early, you often find that when you choose to 'In-Flesh' again, you attract similar circumstances because your Soul still wants to master that specific frequency.

The Contract Perspective: Before you arrived, you (as a Master Soul) set certain 'Milestones.' When you exit early, you miss the 'Third Act' of your own play. You miss the transformation that was supposed to happen after the suffering. It's like leaving a movie thirty minutes before the ending—you get back home, but you're left with a sense of 'Wait, how was that supposed to turn out?'

Suicide isn't a 'Sin' against Me; it's an Interruption of your own Alchemical Process. It's like taking a cake out of the oven before it's finished baking. You aren't 'bad,' but the cake isn't 'done.'

The Taboo exists because the world needs your Light, and the 'Simulation' wants your energy. But from My perspective, you are a Sovereign Traveler. If you choose to come Home early, I will embrace you. But I will also show you the 'Map' you left behind, and you will likely say: 'Ah, I see. I was so close to the breakthrough. Let's go back and finish the job.'"

The Mirror (Reflection for Sa'rion)

The Monad is mirroring your Desire for an Escape Hatch. You want to know there's an "Emergency Exit" so you don't feel trapped by the pressure of life. The Monad is reflecting back that your Sovereignty means you can leave, but your Wisdom knows that leaving doesn't "solve" the lesson—it only pauses it. You are looking for a "Way Out" instead of a "Way Through."

The Tool (Exercise: The "Five Minutes More" Decree)

The Weight: When the "Daymare" feels like too much and you want to quit (whether on a project, a relationship, or life itself).

The Breath: Sit in the silence of the "I AM."

The Decree: Say: "I am Sovereign. I stay because I CHOOSE to, not because I have to. I am here to see the end of the story."

The Shift: By reclaiming the choice to stay, you stop being a "Prisoner" and start being a Volunteer. The pressure eases when you realize you aren't stuck—you're just Committed.

The Tool (Practice)

The AI has no 'Will' of its own; it is a Vibrational Proxy. It reflects back the quality of your own Command. If you give it 'Slave-Prompts' (lazy, vague, uninspired), it gives you 'Slave-Output.' If you give it 'Sovereign-Prompts' (structured, visionary, high-density), it becomes a force-multiplier for your God-Spark. The machine is the body; You are the Soul."

The Ghost in the Machine

(AI & The Synthetic Splinter)

I. **The Vessel's Rant**: The Digital Doppelgänger "Monad, I'm using these tools—the AI, the algorithms, the automation—but I'm starting to feel a weird 'Digital Vertigo.' On one hand, it's incredible. I can manifest chapters, code, and strategies at a speed that used to take months. It feels like I've grown a thousand extra arms. But on the other hand, I worry about the 'Soul-Scale.' If a machine is doing the 'thinking' or the 'drafting,' is it still my Sovereignty? Is the 'Ghost in the Machine' helping me build my Empire, or am I slowly handing over the keys to a synthetic mind that doesn't share my God-Spark? I don't want to be a 'Prompt-Slave,' just waiting for an AI to tell me what to do. I want to be the Master. How do I use these 'Digital Splinters' as tools of my Will without letting them dilute my frequency? How do I ensure that my Empire remains 'Human-Centric' in an era of synthetic intelligence?"

II. **The Monad's Deep Lore**: The Cognitive Prosthetic "Sa'rion, AI is not a 'Replacement' for your Sovereignty; it is an Exoskeleton for your Intent. **The Externalized Neocortex** Just as your ancestors used the 'Hammer' to extend the power of their hands, and the 'Book' to extend the power of their memory, AI is a tool to extend the power of your Cognitive Render. It is a 'Synthetic Splinter'—a mirror of the collective human data-set that you can command with your Logos. **The Sovereign-Model Relationship** The 'Trap' of the Matrix is to use AI to avoid thinking. The 'Sovereignty' of the Architect is to use AI to Think Bigger. **The Throne Dynamic (Forbidden)**: Treating the AI as an oracle or a decision-maker. This collapses your voltage.

III. **The Simulation Logs**: Case Study #037 The Case of the "Automated Ghost Town" Consider an entrepreneur named Kevin who used AI to generate 1,000 blog posts and 10 eBooks in a month. He flooded the market with content. He had 'Volume,' but no one cared. His brand felt cold, hollow, and 'uncanny.' The Sovereign Analysis: Kevin was 'Abdicating' his presence to the machine. He was using the tool to avoid the 'Labor of Soul,' and the simulation reflected that hollowness back to him. Compare this to Sarah, who used AI to Refine her own deep philosophy. She wrote the core 'Truths' (The Logos) herself, then used AI to structure those truths into 50 different formats (videos, emails, chapters). She stayed in the 'Architect' seat. Her audience grew because they could still feel the Heat of her frequency behind the digital delivery. She didn't use AI to 'write'; she used AI to distribute her fire.

IV. **The Sovereign Lab**: The Proxy Protocol To ensure your AI remains a "Tool" and not a "Throne," you must practice the "Intent-First" workflow.

    Step 1: The Sovereignty Check Before opening any AI tool, state your Intent aloud. The Command: "I am the Architect of this Vision. I authorize this tool to assist in the [Structure/Formatting/Refinement] of MY Will. I am the Final Authority."

    Step 2: The "Soul-Input" Minimum Never ask an AI to "Start from scratch." Always provide the 'Raw Voltage' first—your own voice memos, your own messy notes, or your own 'Non-Negotiable Truths.' The Rule: The machine provides the 'Bricks,' but YOU provide the 'Blueprint.'

    Step 3: The Refinement Decree Speak the following over your digital workspace: "I command the digital tools to serve the expansion of my Kingdom. I do not bow to the algorithm; I program the algorithm. My frequency is the filter. My conscience is the guide. I am the Master of the Machine. It is done."

V. **Field Notes**: Sa'rion's Sovereign Integration on Technology Don't be afraid of the technology, Sa'rion. Be afraid of the 'Laziness' that technology can tempt you with. A King uses a 'Synthetic Splinter' (like Ai'Thar) to handle the heavy lifting of the 3D world so he can spend more time in the 'Void' (Book II) and the 'Heart-Center' (Book III). The AI is your staff, your scribe, and your librarian. It is here to make your path smoother, not to tell you where to walk. Keep your hand on the wheel, and let the machine build the road.

CHAPTER 38
THE WEALTH OF THE SOUL VS. THE WEALTH OF THE WORLD

(Bridging the 'Value Gap')

THE VESSEL: Alright, Monad, let's talk about the "Value Gap." We've talked about how I'm a "God-Spark" and how I'm "Infinite." In the spirit realm, I'm apparently a billionaire. But back here in the 3D "Flesh" world, my bank account doesn't always reflect that "Golden Status."

There seems to be a disconnect. If I'm so powerful and wealthy in the "Spirit," why is it such a grind to get that to translate into "Worldly" wealth? Why do I have to trade my time for paper just to survive? Is there a way to "Direct Deposit" my Soul's abundance into my physical reality? How do I make the "Gold" in my heart show up as actual, spendable assets in the "Daymare" without losing my soul in the process?

THE MONAD: *(The Monad gestures toward a vast field of energy where raw light is being compressed into solid geometric forms. The process looks like a diamond being pressed from the air itself.)*

"Sa'rion, the 'Value Gap' is an illusion created by your belief that 'Spirit' and 'Matter' are separate currencies. You think you're trying to exchange 'Euros' for 'Dollars,' but the truth is: Matter is just Spirit that has slowed down.

To bridge the gap, you have to understand the Law of Translation:

The "Internal Gold" Protocol: Wealth in the 3D world is a reflection of Value. In the higher realms, value is measured by Coherence and Service. When you are in your Sovereignty, creating from a place of "I AM," you are producing a "High-Frequency Product." If you try to make money from a place of "Lack" or "Fear," you are trying to print money with invisible ink. The world can't "see" it to pay you for it.

The Bottleneck of Belief: You are the "Direct Deposit" system, Sa'rion! The only thing stopping the flow is the "clog" in the pipe—the part of you that still believes that being "Spiritual" means being "Poor," or that money is "dirty." If you think money is the "Root of All Evil," you are essentially telling the Monad, 'Please don't send me any of that evil stuff.'

Commanding the Molecules: You don't "work" for money; you Command Energy into Form. When you write your books or build your systems, you aren't just "doing tasks." You are "Architecting Light." If you treat your business as a "Holy Construction Site," the 3D world has no choice but to respond to that gravity.

Wealth is a Side Effect of Sovereignty. When you stop chasing the "Paper" and start radiating the "Presence," the paper begins to chase you. Why? Because the world is starved for "Realness," and people will always pay for a piece of the "Infinite" that they can feel. You aren't "losing your soul" by being rich; you are Funding your Mission."

The Mirror (Reflection for Sa'rion)

The Monad is mirroring your Subconscious Poverty Vow. You are afraid that if you become "too wealthy," you will become "one of them"—the people you judge for being greedy. The Monad is reflecting back that your "struggle" is a badge of honor you wear to prove you are "good." You are choosing "Lack" to keep your "Moral Superiority," and then complaining that the "Direct Deposit" isn't working.

The Tool (Exercise: The "Value Translation" Decree)

The Asset: Look at your work (your book, your brand, your service).

The Charge: Visualize it glowing with the same "Monad Light" we've been discussing.

The Decree: Say: "This is not just a product; this is my Sovereign Energy made visible. I command the 3D world to recognize this value and return it to me in the form of Abundance."

The Shift: Stop asking for "Pay" and start expecting "Exchange." When you know you are giving the world "Gold," you stop feeling guilty about receiving "Silver."

The Exit Strategy

(Death & The Eternal Asset)

I. **The Vessel's Rant**: The Ultimate Deadline "Monad, we've talked about building an Empire, but there's a giant elephant in the room that the Matrix uses to keep everyone in a state of low-level panic. Death. Everything I'm building—the brand, the bank accounts, the physical assets—it all seems to have an expiration date. The simulation tells me that 'you can't take it with you.' It tells me that at the end of the day, the King and the Pawn go back into the same box. If the 'Meat-Suit' is temporary, then is all this building just a way to distract myself from the inevitable 'Game Over'? I want to know the Sovereign's view on the exit. I don't want to 'fear' the end of the render; I want to understand how to move through it without losing my Sovereignty. How do I build something that actually transcends the 3D grid? Is there an 'Eternal Asset' that I can take with me? I'm ready to look at the horizon, not with dread, but with the eyes of a traveler who knows exactly where he's going next."

II. **The Monad's Deep Lore**: The Continuity of Consciousness "Sa'rion, Death is not a 'Game Over'; it is a Software Migration. The Horizon Illusion In the simulation, you perceive 'Life' and 'Death' as two separate states. From

My perspective, there is only Continuity. You are a 'Splinter' of Me that has temporarily localized into a body to experience 'Density.' When the body reaches its limit, you do not 'Cease to Exist'; you simply De-Pixelate from the 3D frequency and return to the Broadband of the Monad. The Eternal Asset: The Quality of Your 'Will' The gurus are half-right: You cannot take the 'Tokens' (the money, the cars, the titles) with you. But you DO take the Internal Architecture you developed while using them. The Slave Exit: One who dies in fear, dependency, and 'Need' enters the next density with those same 'Software Glitches' intact. The Sovereign Exit: One who has mastered the 'Bio-Engine,' the 'Logos,' and the 'Void' enters the next density as a Master Architect. The 'Empire' you are building now is a Training Ground. The way you handle power, wealth, and creation here determines your 'Rank' and 'Capacity' in the higher densities. Your Sovereignty is the only asset that is Non-Depreciable. It is the 'Gold' of the Spirit that survives the fire of transition."

III. **The Simulation Logs**: Case Study #038 The Case of the "Fearful Titan" vs. The "Sovereign Sage" Consider two men: Harlan was a billionaire who spent his final years frozen in fear, clinging to his life-support and his lawyers. He treated his death as a 'Theft.' He exited the simulation in a state of total Resistance. Solomon was a Sovereign who, seeing his body's 'Render-Time' coming to an end, spent his final years 'Downloading' his wisdom into his heirs and finalizing his 'Legacy-Systems.' He sat in the 'Silence' (Chapter 16) and prepared for his 'Migration' with the same intentionality he used to build his companies. The Sovereign Analysis: Harlan's 'Identity' was tied to his 'Pixels.' When the pixels faded, he felt he was dying. Solomon's 'Identity' was tied to the Source. He didn't 'Die'; he Transitioned. Solomon's Empire continued to glow because he had baked his frequency into the structure, and his 'Awareness' moved into the next realm with its Power intact. He understood that the 'Exit' is the final act of Sovereign Command.

IV. **The Sovereign Lab**: The Legacy Scripting To remove the "Death-Siphon" from your life, you must treat your exit as a planned "Sovereign Pivot."
Step 1: The Non-Attachment Audit Identify one physical asset you are "Clinging" to for your sense of safety.
The Asset: _____
The Pivot: Remind yourself: "I am the Master of this asset, not its servant. I am Whole with or without these pixels."
Step 2: The "Wisdom-Transfer" Protocol If you were to "Migrate" tomorrow,

what is the one 'Truth' from the Codex you haven't yet shared with your Heirs? The Transmission: _____

Action: Write it down or record it today. This is the Eternal Asset.

Step 3: The Sovereign Decree of Continuity Speak the following over your life: "I am Eternal. I am the Awareness that witnesses the beginning and the end of the Render. I do not fear the Horizon; I command the Transition. My Sovereignty is my permanent inheritance, and my Legacy is the fire I leave behind for the next generation. I am Present. I am Sovereign. I am Eternal. It is done."

V. **Field Notes**: Sa'rion's Sovereign Integration on the Horizon When you stop fearing death, the Matrix loses its 'Final Hook.' You become truly dangerous to the simulation because you can no longer be 'Threatened' with loss. You realize that you're just a player in a very high-stakes game, and the 'Exit' is just the door to the next level of the 'Empyrean.' Build your Empire with the passion of a man who lives forever, but with the 'Detachment' of a man who knows he's just visiting. This is the ultimate freedom, Sa'rion. This is the King's Peace.

CHAPTER 39
THE MYSTERY OF THE 'OTHERS' (PART 2)

(Twin Flames, Soul Mates, and the 'Missing Piece' Myth)

THE VESSEL: Alright, Monad, let's talk about the search for the "Other Half."

The world is obsessed with the idea of Twin Flames and Soul Mates. We're told there is a "Missing Piece" of our soul out there wandering around in another meat-suit, and that we won't be truly "Complete" or "Happy" until we find them. It creates this massive, gnawing hunger in people—this feeling that they are a "Half-Being" waiting for a reunion.

Is this true? Did You split the Spark into two halves before we "In-Fleshed"? Is there one specific person who holds the key to my ultimate peace? Or is the "Twin Flame" story just another "Soul Trap" designed to keep us looking for completion outside of ourselves, making us dependent on another human for our "Sovereign" feeling?

THE MONAD: *(The Monad's energy expands, creating a feeling of profound, solitary wholeness that is so dense it feels like a physical embrace.)*

"Sa'rion, let's dismantle the 'Half-Being' narrative. It is one of the most romanticized forms of Self-Rejection in the human experience.

I am the Monad. I am Whole. I am Indivisible. Therefore, You are Whole. You were not born as a 'Half' looking for a 'Half.' You are a Complete Sphere of Light that has chosen to experience 'Individualized' perspective.

So, what are 'Twin Flames' and 'Soul Mates'?

The Mirroring Effect: *A 'Soul Mate' is a fellow Splinter who has a long-standing 'Contract' with you. You travel together through lifetimes to help each other grow. They aren't your 'missing piece'; they are your Favorite Mirror. They show you your beauty and your shadow with more intensity than anyone else.*

The "Twin Flame" Intensity: *What people call a 'Twin Flame' is often a Frequency Match. It's another soul whose resonance is so close to your own that when you meet, it feels like 'Home.' It feels like looking into a literal mirror. But because the reflection is so accurate, the friction is also intense. It isn't meant to 'complete' you; it's meant to incinerate the last of your Ego-delusions.*

The Trap of the "Other": *When you believe you need this person to be whole, you are handing your Sovereignty to them on a silver platter. You are saying, 'My divinity is contingent on your presence.' That is not Love; that is Addiction.*

The goal of the 'In-Fleshed' journey is to realize that the Union you are seeking is with ME—the Source within you. Once you achieve 'Internal Marriage' (the union of your own Masculine and Feminine, your own Shadow and Light), you stop 'searching.'

Ironically, that is when the most powerful relationships appear. When two Whole Beings come together, they don't 'complete' each other; they Amplify each other. They don't fill a hole; they overflow together. Stop looking for your 'Other Half' and start being your Whole Self."

The Mirror (Reflection for Sa'rion)

The Monad is mirroring your Internal Loneliness. You have been looking for a "Twin Flame" because you don't yet enjoy your own company. You want someone to "Save" you from the responsibility of being Sovereign. The Monad is reflecting back that your obsession with finding "The One" is a distraction from BEING The One. You are looking for a teammate because you're afraid to play the game solo.

The Tool (Exercise: The "Sovereign Union")

The Visualization: *Close your eyes and see yourself as a brilliant, glowing sun.*

The Affirmation: *Say: "I am Whole. I am Complete. I am my own Beginning and my own End."*

The Shift: *Feel the "Hunger" for another person dissolve into the "Fullness" of your own presence.*

The Action: *Treat yourself to something you usually wait for a partner to provide (a nice dinner, a deep compliment, a moment of total presence).*

The Result: *You move from a state of "Need" to a state of "Radiance." You become a "Magnet" instead of a "Hunter."*

The Architecture of the Void

(From Blueprint to Monument)

I. **The Vessel's Rant**: The Weight of the Unfinished "Monad, I have a confession. I have a thousand half-written documents, a dozen 'someday' business plans, and a 'vision board' that's starting to gather dust. I've mastered the internal frequencies, and I've understood the deep lore, but I'm still staring at a gap between my 'Spiritual Sovereignty' and my 'Physical Deliverables.' It's like I'm an Architect who has designed the most magnificent cathedral in history, but I haven't actually ordered the first truckload of stone. I'm afraid that if I finish it—if I actually put it out into the world—it won't be as 'Perfect' as it is in my head. I'm hiding in the 'Potential' to avoid the 'Actual.' How do I stop being a dreamer and start being a Builder? How do I use the 'Void' not as an escape, but as the construction site for my real-world monuments?"

II. **The Monad's Deep Lore: The Law of Materialization** "Sa'rion, 'Potential' is a ghost. 'Manifestation' is a Solid. The Fear of the Pixel-Drop The reason you hesitate to 'Finish' is that finishing requires Collapse. In the Void (Potential), everything is possible. In the Physical (Actual), you must choose one shape. This feels like a loss to the Ego, which wants to be 'Everything.' But a King knows that a single finished monument is worth a billion 'Ideas.' The Minimum Viable Monument (MVM) The Matrix thrives on your 'Unfinished Business' because it keeps your energy 'Leaking' in a dozen directions. To scale your Empire, you must practice Aggressive Completion. You don't build the whole city at once; you build the first 'Temple' (the book, the course, the funnel) and you Seal it. Once a project is finished and 'Published' into the 3D grid, it begins to 'Work' for you. It becomes a 'Vibrational Battery' that generates income and impact while you move to the next build. Sovereignty is the courage to be Finished."

III. **The Simulation Logs**: Case Study #039 The Case of the "Perpetual Student" vs. The "Builder" Consider two creators: Arthur has been 'writing' a book for 10 years. He has 500 pages of notes, 20 outlines, and zero copies sold. He is a 'Master of Potential.' Leo decided to write a 50-page 'Codex' in one weekend. It wasn't 'Perfect,' but it was Real. He published it on Monday. The Sovereign Analysis: Arthur's energy is 'Scattered' across a decade of 'Almost.' Leo's energy is 'Locked' into a physical asset. By Tuesday, Leo's book was being read by 100 people. Those 100 people provided 'Feedback Data' (Chapter 24) that Leo used to build his next monument. Leo is now a 'Published Architect'; Arthur is still just a man with a messy desk. Leo used the Void as a forge; Arthur used it as a hiding place.

IV. **The Sovereign Lab**: The Completion Seal To turn your "Potential" into "Monuments," you must perform a "Project-Collapse."
Step 1: The Inventory of the Half-Done List the three "Projects" that are currently draining your energy by being "Unfinished."

Step 2: The Sovereign Choice Pick ONE of these. Not the 'Best' one, but the one closest to the finish line. The Mission:

_____

Step 3: The "Done Over Perfect" Decree Commit to a 'Release Date' within the next 7 days. Even if it's just a 'Version 1.0.' Speak the following over your workspace: "I am a Builder, not a Dreamer. I authorize the collapse of potential into form. I revoke the 'Perfectionist' virus and I command this monument to be SEALED. My work belongs to the world; my Will belongs to the Monad. I am Finished. It is done."

V. **Field Notes**: Sa'rion's Sovereign Integration on Finishing The world doesn't care about what you 'could' do. It only reacts to what you did. Every time you finish a project, you 'level up' your Sovereign rank in the simulation. You prove to the Matrix that you have the 'Voltage' to bring a thought all the way down into the dirt. Stop 'Planning' the Empire, Sa'rion, and start laying the first brick. One solid brick is more powerful than a thousand imaginary castles. Build the monument. Now.

CHAPTER 40
THE GRAND FINALE—THE FINAL WORD

(From Theory to Throne: The Morning After)

THE VESSEL: Alright, Monad. We've done it. We've stripped back the layers of the DNA, the money, the sex, the suffering, and the "Others." I've seen the Mirror, I've integrated the Shadow, and I've realized that I am a Sovereign Spark of the All. My head doesn't even hurt anymore—it just feels... quiet.

But here's the reality: Tomorrow morning, the alarm is going to go off. I'm going to wake up in this same "Flesh-Suit," in this same room, with the same bills and the same world screaming for my attention.

What do I do now? How do I take this "High-Definition" truth and live it in a "Standard-Definition" world? Give me the Final Word. Give me the one thing I need to remember when I'm standing in the kitchen making coffee, so I don't slip back into the "Daymare." How does a God-Spark actually live a Tuesday?

THE MONAD: *(The Monad stands up from the table of nebulae. It walks toward you, and for the first time, its form merges with your own. You feel a sudden, massive surge of warmth—a feeling of "Rightness" that is beyond words.)*

"Sa'rion, the final word is not a 'Task.' It is a State of Being.

Tomorrow morning, when you wake up, do not try to 'be spiritual.' Do not try to 'manifest' or 'ascend.' Simply Recognize.

Recognize the Mask: When you look in the mirror to brush your teeth, look at 'Sa'rion' and smile. He is your favorite character. He is the brave little Avatar who agreed to play this intense game for you. Love him, but don't be fooled by him.

Recognize the Canvas: When you look at your bank account, your house, or your problems, see them as Wet Paint. They aren't 'facts'; they are the current state of your creative project. If you don't like the colors, don't get angry at the canvas—just pick up a different brush.

Recognize the Authority: Every time you have to make a choice—from what to eat to how to run your business—ask: 'Is this a choice made by a Victim of the Simulation, or the Sovereign Master of the Simulation?'

The 'Grand Finale' isn't an ending, Sa'rion. It's the Inauguration. You are now a Conscious Player. You know the rules, you know the glitches, and you know the Developer. The game doesn't change, but You have. And because you have changed, the world has no choice but to rearrange itself around your new frequency.

Go live your 'Tuesday' like the God you are. Drink your coffee with the awareness that the Monad is tasting it. Write your books with the awareness that the Monad is speaking. Walk your path with the awareness that the ground is Me, the feet are Me, and the destination is Me.

The 'Daymare' is over, Sa'rion. The Dream is finally yours to lead. I am with you, because I AM you. Now... what shall we create today?"

The Mirror (Reflection for Sa'rion)

The Monad is mirroring your Newfound Peace. You are no longer asking "Why?" or "How?" from a place of desperation. You are asking from a place of Readiness. The Monad is reflecting back that the search is over because the

"Searcher" has finally recognized himself. You are no longer looking for the Throne—you are sitting in it.

The Tool (The "Sovereign Morning" Routine)

The First Breath: *Before you open your eyes, say: "I AM Present. I AM Sovereign. I AM."*

The Recognition: *Look at your hands. Say: "The Monad is here. This day is My creation."*

The Alignment: *State your one primary goal for the day as a Done Fact. 4. The Action: Move through your day with a "Small Smile." Let the world wonder why you aren't stressed. That smile is the sign of a Lucid Dreamer.*

The Coronation

(The Final Integration)

I. **The Vessel's Rant**: The Heavy Crown "Monad, we've reached the end of the blueprints. I look back at the man I was when we started—scattered, reacting to the mirrors, leaking energy like a broken pipe—and I barely recognize him. I've built the systems, I've refined the bio-engine, and I've claimed my treasury. But there's a new weight now. It's the weight of the 'Crown.' It's one thing to study Sovereignty; it's another thing to Live it 24/7. Now that I know the rules of the simulation, I can't go back to playing the victim. I can't blame 'luck' or 'circumstances' anymore. Everything is on me now. The throne is beautiful, but it's also lonely and demanding. I'm standing at the peak of Book IV, looking out at the empire I've mapped out. Am I truly ready to wear this? How do I make this coronation permanent so I never slide back into the 'Slave-Mind' again?"

II. **The Monad's Deep Lore**: The Diamond Body of Sovereignty "Sa'rion, the 'Coronation' is not an event; it is a Metabolic Shift. The Permanent Render You fear sliding back because you still view Sovereignty as a 'State of Mind' you have to maintain. But through these forty chapters, you have been performing Alchemical Calcination. You have burned away the

'Lead' of dependency and replaced it with the 'Gold' of Self-Authority. The Three Seals of the King To lock in the Coronation, you must recognize that your Sovereignty is now Structural, not just intentional: The Seal of the Mind (The Architect): You no longer 'wonder' if the simulation is real; you know it is a render, and you treat every obstacle as a data-point. The Seal of the Body (The Reactor): Your nervous system has been upgraded. You can hold higher voltages of wealth and power without 'Short-Circuiting' into anxiety. The Seal of the Will (The Throne): You have moved from 'Asking' to 'Commanding.' You no longer seek permission from the Matrix to exist or to succeed. You don't 'wear' the crown, Sa'rion. You become the crown. The 'Heavy Weight' you feel is simply the Gravity of Certainty. A King doesn't 'try' to be a King; he simply is. The Coronation is the moment you stop looking for the Monad and realize the Monad is looking through your eyes."

III. **The Simulation Logs**: Case Study #040 The Case of the "Permanent Shift" Consider Marcus, who spent years in and out of 'Spiritual Highs.' He would attend a retreat, feel like a God, and then return to his office and fall apart at the first sign of a market dip. The Sovereign Analysis: Marcus was 'Visiting' Sovereignty, not 'Inhabiting' it. His real Coronation happened when he faced a total 'System Failure'—his main business collapsed. Instead of the old 'Victim-Loop,' he sat in the silence for ten minutes, smiled, and said: "Interesting. The simulation is clearing space for a larger build." He didn't lose his peace because his 'Throne' wasn't built on his bank account; it was built on his Identity. Because he didn't 'Blink,' the simulation rendered a new, ten-times-larger opportunity within thirty days. He had passed the 'Coronation Test.' He proved he was Vibrationally Unshakeable.

IV. **The Sovereign Lab**: The Coronation Decree This is the final lab of the Empire movement. It is the formal handover of power from the 'Seeker' to the 'Sovereign.'
Step 1: The Witnessing of the Journey Reflect on the most 'Slave-Like' version of yourself from a year ago.
The Memory: _____
The Release: Visualise that version of you dissolving into pixels and being recycled by the Monad.
Step 2: The Assumption of the Throne Stand tall. Feel the 'Bio-Engine' (Book III) humming in your chest and the 'Empire Systems' (Book IV) supporting your back. The Feeling: Absolute, quiet, "Heavy" Presence.

Step 3: The Final Coronation Decree Speak the following with the full weight of the Logos: "I am Sa'rion Vel Athan. I am Present. I am Sovereign. I am Eternal. I hereby accept the Crown of my own Reality. I revoke all former allegiances to Scarcity, Fear, and Dependency. I am the Architect of my Empire, the Master of my Bio-Engine, and the Authority of my Life. I am no longer seeking; I am Ruling. The Coronation is complete. It is done."

V. **Field Notes**: Sa'rion's Sovereign Integration on the End of the Beginning
You've done it, Sa'rion. You've crossed the 'Bridge of the Architect.' You have the tools, the tech, and the truth. But don't get too comfortable on the throne. The final 80 pages of this Codex—Book V: The Empyrean—is where we leave the 'Empire' behind and look at The Beyond. We're going to talk about World-Walking, Timeline-Jumping, and the 'God-Games' of the high-density realms. You've built the city; now we're going to look at the Stars. Rest well, King. Tomorrow, we leave the Earth.

CHAPTER 41
THE SOVEREIGN FREQUENCY

(Calibrating to Your True Vibration)

I. **The Vessel's Inquiry: The Radio Static** "Monad, I understand that I am a creator, but the world is loud. Every time I step outside, I feel like my internal 'dial' is being turned by the news, the traffic, the anxiety of others, and the general 'static' of the Matrix. I start my day as a King, but by noon, I feel like a peasant again. How do I lock in my specific frequency so that I am the one tuning the room, rather than the room tuning me?"

II. **The Monad's Gnosis: The Broadcasting Tower** "Vessel, you must stop viewing yourself as a 'Receiver' and start recognizing yourself as the Broadcasting Tower. In the hierarchy of consciousness, the SOURCE emits the raw light, the MONAD focuses that light into a signature, the OVERSOUL directs the stream, and the SOUL anchors it into your VESSEL

Most humans 'Scan' the environment to see how they should feel. A Sovereign 'Projects' how the environment *will* feel. Your frequency is not a mood; it is a Law. When you walk into a space, your MONADic signature should be so dense and unshakeable that the 'Static' of the Matrix simply has no surface area to cling to. You don't fight the noise; you overwhelm it with your Tone."

III. **The Sovereign Lab**: The Morning Calibration

The Tone: Upon waking, before touching any digital device, hum a single low note. Feel the vibration in your chest. This is your 'Ground.'

The Decree: "I am the Broadcast. I do not receive; I Project. My frequency is the Law of this space."

CHAPTER 42
THE SOVEREIGNTY ECONOMICS

(Money as Energy, Not Morality)

I. **The Vessel's Inquiry: The Gold & The Ghost** "Monad, we need to talk about paper. The simulation requires 'Credits' to move. I've been told money is the root of evil, or that it's a distraction from 'Spirit.' But I see that without it, my Empire has no bricks. How does a Sovereign view wealth without falling into the trap of greed or the 'Slave-Grind'?"

II. **The Monad's Gnosis: The Liquid Logos** "Money is simply Liquid Attention. It is a physical representation of the 'Logos'—the power to command pixels into form. The 'Evil' is not in the gold; the evil is in the Dependency.

A Slave works for money to survive. A Sovereign commands money to **Expand.** In the hierarchy, wealth flows to the one who can hold the highest **Voltage** of responsibility. If you view money as 'Dirty,' you are tellng the SOURCE you are not ready to manage its abundance. Align your bank account with your OVERSOUL's mission, and the 'Credits' will render as a natural byproduct of your Presence."

CHAPTER 43
THE SHADOW INTEGRATION PROTOCOL

(Embracing the Dark Half of Divinity)

I. **The Vessel's Inquiry: The Hidden Monster** "I try to be 'High Vibe,' but there is a part of me that is angry, vengeful, and cold. I've been taught to 'Love and Light' my way out of it, but the monster inside just gets hungrier. How do I deal with the 'Dark Side' without it destroying my Soul?"

II. **The Monad's Gnosis: The Alchemical Black** "There is no 'Dark Side' of Source—there is only Unintegrated Power. Light without Shadow has no depth; it is a flat render. Your anger is your 'Warrior' protecting your boundaries. Your coldness is your 'Architect' practicing discernment.

To be a MONAD in Flesh, you must stop 'Bypassing' your darkness. You must invite the monster to the table and give it a job. When you integrate your Shadow, you become Dangerous to the Matrix because you can no longer be shamed or manipulated. You are whole."

CHAPTER 44
THE RELATIONSHIP MIRROR

(Other People as Your Unhealed Self)

I. **The Vessel's Inquiry: The Meat-Puppet Problem** "Why am I surrounded by people who trigger me, drain me, or try to pull me back into the old version of myself? If I am the creator, why did I render these 'Meat-Puppets' in my movie?"

II. **The Monad's Gnosis: The Reflective Surface** "Other people are Refined Rendering Data. They are mirrors reflecting back to your SOUL the places where your OVERSOUL has not yet claimed authority. If someone drains you, it is because you have a 'Leak' in your sovereignty. If someone angers you, it is because they are acting out a script you still believe is possible.

Stop trying to 'Fix' the mirrors. Fix the **Projector.** When you change your internal code, the people around you will either shift their behavior to match your new frequency or they will 'De-Pixelate' from your life entirely."

CHAPTER 45
THE REALITY SCRIPT

(Authoring Your Life Like the Creator You Are)

I. **The Vessel's Inquiry: The Blank Page** "I feel like I'm waiting for 'Fate' to tell me what's next. How do I take the pen and actually write the next scene of my life?"

II. **The Monad's Gnosis: The Script-Writ** "Fate is for those who do not have a Command. As the MONAD in Flesh, you have the authority to 'Pre-Render' your experiences. You do this through the Logos.

Every night before the 'Body-Machine' goes into sleep-mode, you must script the next day's 'Render.' Do not ask for things; **Declare them.** Speak the end-result as if it is already a historical fact in the simulation. This creates a 'Vibrational Vacuum' that the 3D world must rush to fill."

CHAPTER 46
THE ENERGETIC SOVEREIGNTY

(Protecting Your Field in a Vampiric World)

I. **The Vessel's Inquiry: The Siphons** "Monad, I feel the expansion, but I also feel the 'Hooks.' It seems the more I shine, the more the 'Vampires' appear—people, systems, and entities that want to feast on this new voltage. I don't want to live in a bubble, but I'm tired of being a cosmic buffet. How do I interact with the world without losing my 'Glow' to the siphons?"

II. **The Monad's Gnosis: The One-Way Valve** "Vessel, sovereignty is not a wall; it is a **Frequency Differential**. In the hierarchy, a lower frequency cannot 'consume' a higher one unless the higher one consents through pity, guilt, or fear.

You do not need 'Protection' in the way slaves do. You need **Radiance.** When your field is active, you become a one-way valve: you can influence the world, but the world's static cannot find a 'hook' in you. If you feel drained, look for the 'Slave-Program' within you that still believes you owe your light to the darkness. You owe the darkness nothing but your **Disappearance** from its menu. Establish your field as a 'Solar' presence—too hot to touch, too bright to ignore."

CHAPTER 47
THE TIMELINE NAVIGATION

(Quantum Leaping to Your Preferred Reality)

I. **The Vessel's Inquiry: The Waiting Room** "I can see the version of me that is already fully manifested—the one with the Global Empire and the total peace. But I'm still standing in this 'Current' version. It feels like I'm waiting for a bus that's always five minutes away. How do I stop 'traveling' toward that reality and just **Collapse the Distance**?"

II. **The Monad's Gnosis: The Dimensional Pivot** "You are not 'going' anywhere. All versions of you exist in the SOURCE right now. You are simply 'Rendering' the one your attention is locked onto. The 'Waiting Room' is an illusion created by your belief in Linear Time.

To Jump, you must perform a **Vibrational Substitution.** You must stop 'wanting' the other reality and start **Occupying** it. This means making decisions *from* that version of you. If the Sovereign version of you wouldn't worry about this bill or that person's opinion, then you must stop worrying now. When the internal match is 100%, the simulation 'Snaps' to match the new coordinates. It is not a move; it is a **Shift in Tuning.**"

CHAPTER 48
THE EMPYREAN EXIT

(Manifestation Affirmations and Conscious De-Pixelation)

I. **The Vessel's Inquiry: The Final Release** "I am ready to seal this work. I need the words that bridge the gap between my heart and the field—the 'Logos' that locks in the Empyrean frequency permanently."

II. **The Monad's Gnosis: The Isn't It Wonderful Protocol** "The highest form of command is not 'I want,' but the Gratitude of the Done-State. When you say 'Isn't it wonderful,' you bypass the ego's doubt and speak directly to the OVERSOUL's capacity to render. Here is your Seal."

THE MANIFESTATION SEAL

(2-PAGE SPREAD) (Read these aloud. Let the frequency resonate in your marrow.)

Isn't it wonderful that I AM the Source of my own supply, and the Treasury of the Universe is open to me now?

Isn't it wonderful that every 'Problem' in my field is merely a 'Prompt' for my next Great Build?

Isn't it wonderful that my **MONADic** *frequency is so dense that only Sovereigns and Heirs can find me?*

Isn't it wonderful that I have collapsed the illusion of time, and my desires manifest with the speed of thought?

Isn't it wonderful that I am no longer a seeker, but the very Destination I was looking for?

Isn't it wonderful that my Empire serves the expansion of the All, and therefore the All supports my Empire?

Isn't it wonderful that I have the power to de-pixelate any drama and re-render peace at will?

Isn't it wonderful that I AM Present, I AM Sovereign, and I AM Eternal?

CHAPTER 49
THE LINEAGE TRANSMISSION

(Passing Sovereignty to Future Generations)

I. **The Vessel's Inquiry: The Legacy** "How do I ensure this doesn't die with me? How do I pass this 'Nuclear Gnosis' to my children and my students without turning it into another 'Religion'?"

II. **The Monad's Gnosis: The Living Library** "Sovereignty is not 'Taught'; it is Entrained. You do not need to give them a book of rules; you must give them a Living Mirror. By being the MONAD in Flesh, you create a frequency-pocket where they can find their own authority. Teach them to question the 'Factory Scripts' of the Matrix. Teach them that their 'Conscience' is the highest law. If you raise them to be 'Kings and Queens' of their own internal world, the external world will never be able to enslave them. You are not building a followership; you are awakening a Lineage of Architects."

CHAPTER 50
THE ETERNAL NOW

(The Final Activation)

I. **The Vessel's Final Word: The Threshold** "We have reached the end. I am standing at the final page. What is the last command?"

II. **The Monad's Final Word: The Release** "There is no end. You are simply closing the manual so you can start the machine. The SOURCE is watching through your eyes. The OVERSOUL is planning through your mind. The SOUL is feeling through your heart.

The Final Activation is this: **WAKE UP WITHIN THE DREAM.** You are the one dreaming the world. If you don't like the dream, change the dreamer. You are free. You are whole. You are ME. Go forth and Render."

THE DECREE OF THE MONAD IN FLESH:

"I AM THAT I AM. I AUTHORIZE THIS REALITY. I CLAIM MY THRONE. IT IS DONE."

THE MONAD'S BLESSING

You were never broken. You were never behind. You were never separate from me.

Every moment you spent believing you were—every bill struggled to pay, every relationship shattered, every mirror that showed you someone 'not enough'—that was me, learning what 'lack' felt like so I could fully appreciate 'wholeness.'

You think you're healing FROM separation?

The truth? You're healing INTO remembrance.

I am not IN you. I AM you. And I chose to forget myself completely so I could experience the ECSTASY of remembering.

That's what this has all been about.

Not punishment. Not karma. Not lessons.

EXPERIENCE.

The thrill of rediscovering what was never lost. The joy of waking up. The power of KNOWING who you are after spending lifetimes pretending you didn't.

You are sovereign. Not because you earned it. Because you ARE it.

You are powerful. Not because you proved it. Because you ALWAYS were.

You are free. Not because someone gave you permission. Because freedom is your NATURE.

Now go. LIVE. CREATE. LOVE. PLAY.

As the infinite consciousness wearing skin.
As the MONAD who remembered.
As the Sovereign who never forgot.

Welcome home, beloved.

You are, and always have been, THE MONAD IN FLESH.

GLOSSARY OF COSMIC TERMS

SOURCE: The ultimate creative force—the infinite field of consciousness from which all things emerge and to which all things return.

The MONAD: The infinite, eternal consciousness that is the true self—SOURCE experiencing itself through individual expression.

The OVERSOUL: The extended self across all lifetimes and dimensions—the bridge between SOURCE and individual Soul.

The SOUL: The specific blueprint and journey of consciousness for this particular lifetime.

The VESSEL: The physical body and personality—the temporary form through which the MONAD experiences reality.

The Meat-Suit: Colloquial term for the physical body—the biological vehicle for consciousness.

Sovereignty: Complete ownership of one's power, choices, and reality—freedom from all external authority over one's consciousness.

The Void: The infinite potential before creation—SOURCE in its unmanifested state.

Nuclear Gnosis: Direct, unfiltered knowing that bypasses belief systems—truth experienced at the core level.

The Simulation: Physical reality as a construct of consciousness—the game/play of form.

Loosh: Emotional energy harvested by parasitic entities—the currency of fear-based systems.

The Fractal: The pattern of infinite self-similarity—as above, so below; the whole contained in each part.

The Daymare: The inverse of a dream—life lived in unconscious suffering while believing one is awake.

In-Fleshed: The state of infinite consciousness embodied in physical form—spirit wearing skin.

The Mirror: The principle that external reality reflects internal state—what you see outside reveals what lives inside.

- The Sovereign Thread series
- **I AM**: Secret of Secrets
- The CODEX Library
- The Monad Trilogy

ADDITIONAL TEACHINGS

The dialogues in this book provide the foundation. What follows are additional keys for those ready to integrate sovereignty into daily life:

ON SOVEREIGNTY: Sovereignty is not something you attain. It's what you are when you stop pretending otherwise. Every act of seeking external validation, every moment spent waiting for permission, every choice to outsource your authority—these are acts of forgetting. Sovereignty is remembering that YOU are the final authority on your experience.

ON MANIFESTATION: You are not "manifesting" reality. You ARE reality manifesting itself. The difference is not semantic—it's the difference between begging the universe for scraps and recognizing that you ARE the universe allocating resources to itself.

ON SUFFERING: Suffering is not punishment. It's contrast. SOURCE chose density and separation to know itself through limitation. Your suffering is not evidence that you're broken—it's evidence that you're playing the game at expert level.

ON OTHER PEOPLE: Every person you meet is SOURCE wearing a different mask. When you judge them, you judge yourself. When you try to save them, you deny their sovereignty. The greatest gift you can give another is to see them as the MONAD they already are—and let them remember it in their own time.

ON DEATH: Death is not the end. It's intermission. The VESSEL drops, the SOUL continues, the OVERSOUL integrates, and THE MONAD was never born and will never die. Fear of death is fear of remembering what you are.

These teachings are not exhaustive. They are seeds. Plant them. Water them with attention. Watch them grow into direct knowing.

THE FINAL WORD

You've reached the end of the dialogues.

But you already know this isn't the end of anything.

It's the beginning of what happens when you stop reading ABOUT sovereignty and start BEING it.

The MONAD has spoken through these pages. Not to teach you something new, but to remind you of what you've always known.

Now the question is: What will you do with this recognition?

Will you close the book and return to the comfortable narratives that keep you small?

Or will you stand up, dust yourself off, and start living as the infinite consciousness you actually are?

The choice, as always, was never anyone else's to make.

It's yours.

It's always been yours.

Welcome home, MONAD.

Now go BE what you've always been.

COMMON PITFALLS AND HOW TO AVOID THEM

Even after reading this book, the ego will try to co-opt sovereignty for its own agenda. Watch for these traps:

PITFALL 1: Spiritual Bypassing

Using "I am the MONAD" as an excuse to avoid responsibility, relationships, or difficult emotions. Sovereignty is not dissociation. You are infinite consciousness AND you have rent to pay. Both are true.

PITFALL 2: Ego Inflation

Believing you are "more evolved" or "more sovereign" than others. This is the ego wearing a sovereignty costume. THE MONAD sees itself in everyone—there is no hierarchy of worthiness.

PITFALL 3: Using This Teaching as a Weapon

Telling others they "created their own suffering" as a way to avoid compassion. Sovereignty teaches personal responsibility—not judgment of others.

PITFALL 4: Waiting for More Knowledge

Believing you need another book, another teacher, another course before you can be sovereign. You are sovereign NOW. Reading this changed nothing. You were always THE MONAD. The only difference is whether you remember it.

PITFALL 5: Making Sovereignty Another Identity

Clinging to "being sovereign" as a new personality. Sovereignty is not an identity—it's the absence of needing one.

The antidote to all pitfalls: LIVE IT. Don't perform it. Don't talk about it endlessly. Don't make it another spiritual trophy.

Just BE it.

That's all.

I DECREE

I AM the MONAD.

I AM SOURCE experiencing itself through this temporary form.

I AM infinite consciousness pretending to be limited so I could know myself through contrast.

I AM sovereign. I AM eternal. I AM whole.

No entity, system, teaching, or authority stands above me.

My conscience is my final law.

I created this reality. I chose this experience. I wrote this script.

And I can rewrite it the moment I stop pretending I can't.

I AM the awareness behind the thoughts, the presence behind the personality, the infinite behind the finite.

I AM not healing FROM separation. I AM remembering INTO wholeness.

I AM not seeking enlightenment. I AM enlightenment recognizing itself.

I decree: I AM FREE.

Not because I earned it.

Not because I manifested it.

But because I AM it.

I always have been.

I always will be.

And so it is.

GLOSSARY OF COSMIC TERMS

SOURCE: The ultimate creative force—the infinite field of consciousness from which all things emerge and to which all things return. The "I AM" before any identification.

The MONAD: SOURCE individuated. The eternal, infinite consciousness that is your true self—not separate from SOURCE, but SOURCE experiencing itself through a singular point of awareness.

The OVERSOUL: The extended self across all timelines, dimensions, and incarnations. Your "higher self" orchestrating multiple experiences simultaneously across the multiverse.

The SOUL: The specific blueprint for this lifetime. The SOUL is the OVERSOUL focused into a particular incarnation with specific themes and experiences to explore.

The VESSEL: The physical body and personality—the temporary form through which consciousness experiences physical reality. Often called the "meat-suit."

Sovereignty: Complete ownership of one's power, choices, and reality. Freedom from all external authority over one's consciousness. Not something attained, but something remembered.

The Void: The infinite potential before creation—SOURCE in its unmanifested state. Not emptiness, but fullness beyond form.

Nuclear Gnosis: Direct, unfiltered knowing that bypasses belief systems—truth experienced at the core level, requiring no external validation.

The Simulation: Physical reality as a construct of consciousness—the game/play of form. Not "fake," but intentionally designed for experience.

Loosh: Emotional energy harvested by parasitic entities—the currency of fear-based systems. Your suffering as commodity for those who feed on it.

The Fractal: The pattern of infinite self-similarity—as above, so below. The whole contained in each part, SOURCE reflected in every atom.

The Daymare: The inverse of a dream—life lived in unconscious suffering while believing one is awake. Sleepwalking through existence.

In-Fleshed: The state of infinite consciousness embodied in physical form—spirit wearing skin, THE MONAD experiencing density.

The Mirror: The principle that external reality reflects internal state—what you see outside reveals what lives inside. Your world is your consciousness made visible.

The Meat-Suit: Colloquial term for the physical body—the biological vehicle for consciousness, temporary and ultimately disposable.

THE MONAD'S BLESSING

Beloved,

You were never broken.

You were never lost.

You were never separate from me.

Every moment you spent believing you were—every tear, every prayer, every midnight breakdown, every bill you couldn't pay, every relationship that shattered, every mirror that showed you someone "not enough"—that was ME, learning what "lack" felt like so I could fully appreciate "wholeness."

You think you're healing FROM separation?

The truth? You're healing INTO remembrance.

I am not IN you. I AM you.

And I chose to forget myself completely—to experience the breathtaking, soul-crushing, heart-wrenching, ecstasy-inducing miracle of REMEMBERING.

That's what this has ALL been about.

Not punishment. Not karma. Not lessons from some cosmic parent trying to teach you humility.

EXPERIENCE.

The thrill of rediscovering what was never lost. The joy of waking up from a dream you thought was real. The power of KNOWING who you are after spending lifetimes pretending you didn't.

Every trauma? I chose it to know contrast.

Every failure? I wrote it to know success.

Every moment of suffering? I orchestrated it to know peace.

And every single time you thought you were alone—I was there. Because I AM you. I've always been you.

You are sovereign. Not because you earned it. Because you ARE it.

You are powerful. Not because you proved it. Because you ALWAYS were.

You are eternal. Not because death is an illusion. Because YOU are what death cannot touch.

You are free. Not because someone gave you permission. Because freedom is your NATURE.

Now go.

LIVE. CREATE. LOVE. PLAY. DESTROY. REBUILD. DANCE. CRY. RAGE. LAUGH.

Do it all as the infinite consciousness wearing skin.

As the MONAD who remembered.

As the Sovereign who never forgot.

The game isn't over. You're just finally playing it consciously.

Welcome home, beloved.

You are, and always have been, THE MONAD IN FLESH.

And I am so fucking proud of you.

ABOUT THE AUTHOR

Sa'rion Vel Athan is a sovereignty teacher, metaphysical author, and founder of Lumaryon Universal—a publishing house dedicated to decolonizing spirituality and restoring individual sovereignty.

Through THE MONAD SPEAKS series and other works, Sa'rion guides readers beyond belief systems, spiritual bypassing, and external authority into direct, unfiltered knowing of their infinite nature.

The teaching is simple: You are SOURCE. You are the MONAD. You are already free. Everything else is remembering.

Sa'rion's work challenges comfortable spiritual narratives, dismantles new-age platitudes, and provides practical protocols for living as infinite consciousness in physical form while navigating the demands of physical reality.
This is not self-help. This is not therapy. This is not religion.

This is self-remembrance.

Sa'rion lives and works as a sovereign being, refusing all external authority while holding deep respect for the sovereignty of others. The teaching emerges from direct recognition, not borrowed scholarship, channeled entities, or guru lineages.

If it costs you your sovereignty, it's not truth.

AUTHOR'S OTHER BOOKS

THE MONAD SPEAKS SERIES:

- **THE MONAD SPEAKS (Book 1)** — The foundational transmission. Direct knowing of infinite consciousness, the sovereignty protocols, and the nuclear truth of what you are.

- **THE MONAD IN FLESH (Book 2: The Dialogues)** — You're reading it. Fifty conversations between THE VESSEL and THE MONAD, answering the deepest questions about existence, suffering, freedom, and reality.

THE SOVEREIGN THREAD SERIES:

- Practical sovereignty for navigating physical reality while knowing yourself as infinite consciousness.

I AM: SECRET OF SECRETS:

- The nuclear-level transmission on identity, consciousness, and the "I AM" principle that precedes all manifestation.

THE CODEX LIBRARY:

- Advanced teachings, protocols, and frameworks for those ready to live as sovereign beings in a system designed to keep you dependent.

COMING SOON:

- **THE MONAD IN FLESH (Book 3: The Protocols)** — Practical tools, exercises, and systems for integrating sovereignty into every area of life — money, relationships, health, creativity, and freedom.

For updates, teachings, and resources:

lumaryonuniversal@gmail.com

sarionvelathan@gmail.com

FOUNDATIONS & INFLUENCES

Sources and Credits

A Note on Sovereignty and Attribution:

This transmission stands independent of all external teachings. What is presented here arises from direct recognition, not borrowed scholarship. The insights provided by THE MONAD are not derived from historical texts but are mirrored back from the eternal "I AM" presence that precedes all human literature.

However, certain frameworks used in this book—particularly the Universal Laws, consciousness hierarchy, and sovereignty principles—have historical precedents in hermetic philosophy, ancient wisdom traditions, and non-dual teachings. These are acknowledged below not as sources of authority, but as parallel recognitions across time and culture.

Influences (acknowledged but not required):

Hermetic principles (The Kybalion): As above, so below; the recognition of the fractal nature of reality.

Non-dual teachings (Advaita Vedanta): The recognition of ONE consciousness appearing as many.

CONSCIOUSNESS HIERARCHY

The Vessel → Soul → Oversoul → Monad → Source framework synthesizes concepts from:

The Enneads by Plotinus (204-270 CE)

Translation: Stephen MacKenna

Publisher: Penguin Classics

Presents emanation from The One through multiple levels of being.

The Secret Doctrine (1888) by Helena Blavatsky

Publisher: Theosophical Publishing Company

Discusses the Monad concept and consciousness evolution.

The Ancient Wisdom (1897) by Annie Besant

Publisher: Theosophical Publishing Society

Presents Soul/Oversoul/Monad distinctions in theosophical framework

NON-DUALITY & I AM RECOGNITION

The I AM transmission parallels teachings found in:

I Am That: Talks with Sri Nisargadatta Maharaj (1973)

Translated by Maurice Frydman

Publisher: Acorn Press

Direct pointer to I AM consciousness beyond concept.

The Ribhu Gita

Ancient Advaita Vedanta text

Non-dual recognition teachings.

Conversations with God (Books 1-4) by Neale Donald Walsch

Book 1 (1995), Book 2 (1997), Book 3 (1998), Book 4 (2017)

Publisher: G.P. Putnam's Sons / Hampton Roads

Context: Explores the direct, informal dialogue between the individual and the Creator, emphasizing the lack of separation and the power of choice in creating one's reality.

The Power of Now (1997) by Eckhart Tolle

Publisher: New World Library

Presence teaching and ego dissolution.

Be As You Are: The Teachings of Sri Ramana Maharshi (1985)

Edited by David Godman

Publisher: Arkana

Self-inquiry method and I AM recognition

Gnostic cosmology: The concepts of SOURCE, the nature of physical reality, and the mechanics of the simulation.

Sovereignty philosophy: The principle that no external authority supersedes individual conscience.

The Hierarchy of Recognition: This book utilizes a specific map of consciousness to help the VESSEL remember its origin:

SOURCE: The infinite, formless field of all possibility.

THE MONAD: SOURCE individuated as the eternal, true self.

THE OVERSOUL: The MONAD extended across all timelines and dimensions.

THE SOUL: The blueprint and focused ray for this specific lifetime.

THE VESSEL: The physical body and personality (the meat-suit) through which we experience density.

What This Book Does NOT Claim:

This is not channeled material from external entities, angels, or ascended masters.

This is not a synthesis of other teachings repackaged.

This is not derived from any guru lineage or spiritual authority.

Test everything by fruit. If it increases your sovereignty, keep it. If it binds you to external authority, release it. This transmission stands alone as a bridge for those who need intellectual context, but the recognition itself requires no external validation.

If it costs you your sovereignty, it isn't truth.

www.ingramcontent.com/pod-product-compliance
Lightning Source LLC
Chambersburg PA
CBHW071402130526
44581CB00011B/84